CW00704184

POLICY AND PRACTICE IN HEALTH AND SOCIAL CARE
NUMBER SIXTEEN

Adoption & Fostering in Scotland

POLICY AND PRACTICE IN HEALTH AND SOCIAL CARE

POLICY AND PRACTICE IN HEALTH AND SOCIAL CARE
SERIES EDITORS
JOYCE CAVAYE and ALISON PETCH

Adoption & Fostering in Scotland

Dr Gary Clapton
Senior Lecturer, Social Work,
School of Social and Political Science,
University of Edinburgh
and
Pauline Hoggan

with a chapter by
Maggie Mellon

Published by
Dunedin Academic Press Ltd
Hudson House
8 Albany Street
Edinburgh EH1 3QB
Scotland

ISBN: 978–1–906716–35–6
ISSN 1750–1407

First published 2012

© 2012 Gary Clapton, Pauline Hoggan and Dunedin Academic Press

*The right of Gary Clapton, Pauline Hoggan and Maggie Melon to be identified
as the authors of this work has been asserted by them in accordance with sections
77 and 78 of the Copyright, Designs and Patents Act 1988*

Crown Copyright material is reproduced by permission of the Controller of
HMSO and the Queen's Printer for Scotland.

All rights reserved.
No part of this publication may be reproduced or transmitted in any form or
by any means or stored in any retrieval system of any nature without prior
written permission, except for fair dealing under the Copyright, Designs
and Patents Act 1988 or in accordance with the terms of a licence issued by
the Copyright Licensing Society in respect of photocopying or reprographic
reproduction. Full acknowledgment as to author, publisher and source must
be given. Application for permission for any other use of copyright material
should be made in writing to the publisher.

British Library Cataloguing in Publication data
A catalogue record for this book is available at the British Library

Typeset by Makar Publishing Production
Printed in Great Britain by CPI Antony Rowe

CONTENTS

SERIES EDITORS' INTRODUCTION

Adoption and fostering are powerful interventions in the lives of children. They are complex processes, life-changing and long-lasting in nature for children who are unable to be cared for by their biological families. Societal changes have seen the demise of the traditional model of adoption, whereby babies were voluntarily given up for adoption by birth parents. Today, there are fewer babies available for adoption or fostering, and children who need new homes tend to be older and have been taken away from their birth parents. Overall, the number of children in the care of local authorities, family, foster or residential care has increased.

This book reflects critically on the significant features of current policy and the practice context of these essential services for children and families. It discusses recent legislation, which introduced comprehensive changes designed to modernise and improve existing adoption and fostering services. The aim was to create a child-centred, flexible system that provides more security for vulnerable children and supports all parties involved in the adoption and fostering process.

Drawing on their own experience of adoption and fostering practice, the authors explore the changing ideology and research base that underpins recent developments and consider complex issues such as Permanence Orders and kinship care. The voices of service users are used to strengthen examples of best practice, which together should inspire practitioners to 'get it right for every child'.

Adoption & Fostering in Scotland moves behind the policy rhetoric to recognise and explore some of the challenges of current policy and practice. The result is an informed and empirically supported review, which extends our understanding of and offers insights into what it means to be a child in care. This volume provides invaluable resources and advice for students and practitioners who aspire to

deliver high-quality child-centred care to the children and families
with whom they work.

Dr Joyce Cavaye   Professor Alison Petch
Faculty of Health and Social Care,   *The Institute for Research and*
The Open University in Scotland,   *Innovation in Social Services (IRISS),*
Edinburgh   *Glasgow*

GLOSSARY OF ABBREVIATIONS

BAAF	British Association for Adoption & Fostering
DCSF	Department for Children, Schools and Families (England and Wales)
FGC	Family Group Conference
FRG	Family Rights Group
GIRFEC	Getting It Right For Every Child
GRO	General Register Office
HMIE	Her Majesty's Inspectorate of Education
IRO	Independent Reviewing Officer
LAAC	Looked After and Accommodated Child
PIU	Performance and Innovation Unit
PO	Permanence Order
SCCYP	Scotland's Commissioner of Children and Young People
SCIE	Social Care Institute for Excellence
SCSWIS	Social Care and Social Work Improvement Scotland
SCRA	Scottish Children's Reporter Administration
SSD	Social Service Department
SWIA	Social Work Inspection Agency

INTRODUCTION

This book is for practitioners and those who wish to practise in the field of adoption and fostering. It will also be invaluable to those who use adoption and fostering services. The book sets out the main contemporary social, practice, policy, legislative and research contexts and issues.

The challenges and opportunities in adoption and fostering in Scotland are much the same as elsewhere in the UK, especially in developing practices such as improving outcomes for children adopted from local authority care, professionalising foster care, post-adoption information exchanges, and incorporating birth parents in support services. Equally so, research findings are applicable across borders: for example, recognition of the need for sensitisation of foster parents to the challenges in caring for a child that has been sexually abused; and the needs of post-care adults.

A Scottish body of knowledge applicable is somewhat thinner on the ground and it is to be hoped that, as a distinct Scottish social work identity develops, this will be informed by adoption and fostering research here. However, at present it is fair to say that writing by Scottish practitioners and researchers, as reflected for example in contributions to *Adoption & Fostering*, has some ground to make up.

The last book on Scottish adoption and fostering was published nearly ten years ago and this was an anthology of articles previously published in *Adoption & Fostering*; in some cases, these dated from the early 1980s (Hill, 2002a). The present book builds on the introduction to *Shaping Child Care Practice in Scotland* (Hill, 2002a) and where relevant Hill's other contributions to the anthology (2002b, 2002c, 2002d). Other uniquely Scottish publications that we have drawn upon extensively include: the Adoption Policy Review Group's reports — *Adoption Policy Review Group — Report Phase I* (Scottish Executive, 2002) and *Adoption: Better Choices for Our children* (Scottish Executive, 2005); the first official review of adoption and fostering in Scotland (*The quality of fostering and adoption services in Scotland,* Scottish Commission for the Regulation of Care, 2007), *Looked After Children and Young People: We Can and Must Do Better* (Scottish Executive, 2007), the Social Work Inspection Agency's report, *Extraordinary Lives — Creating a Positive Future for Looked After Children and Young People in Scotland* (SWIA, 2006); *Moving Forward in Kinship and Foster Care* (Scottish Government, 2008c); and *Guidance on Looked After Children (Scotland) Regulations 2009 and the Adoption and Children (Scotland) Act 2007* (Scottish Government, 2011a). As can be seen from this brief list, there has been a burgeoning of official adoption and fostering-related publications some of which are lengthy documents — the latter *Guidance* (Scottish Government, 2011a) runs to some 216 pages. This is part of a wider trend that poses challenges to practitioners and managers.

Action for Children has critically commented on UK governments' initiatives in what it has called policy 'churn', noting:

> there have been over 400 different initiatives, strategies, funding streams, legislative acts and structural changes to services affecting children and young people over the past 21 years. This is equivalent to over 20 different changes faced by children's services for every year since 1987 ... Half of the developments identified began in the past six years. Three-quarters have come in the past 10 years. (Action for Children, 2009)

The Scottish picture is no different. Hothersall cites thirty pieces of legislation and forty-three policy initiatives since 2000, all of which have a bearing to a greater or lesser extent on children and families practice (Hothersall, 2008, pp. 24–5).

It remains to be seen whether such activity will generate practice gains and better outcomes for the children and families involved. Tarara and Daniel suggest:

> Scotland is in a stock-taking phase, when reform programmes and new frameworks are playing an important role in current policy-making on behalf of children. Research over the last decade has been preoccupied with the workings of the

system and the roles of practitioners. The evidence accumu-
lated provides the ideal platform for a new decade of research
that focuses not so much on what people do, but on how well
they do it. (Tarara and Daniel, 2007)

Whilst there have been many other related publications that contain
material of some relevance to this book — too many to mention at
this point — it is hoped that all salient points have been covered. The
proof of the pudding will be in the book's ultimate value to practitioners, and the service users with whom they work.

Fostering and adoption defined

What follows are essentially official definitions of fostering and adoption. However, we must remember that 'there are few greater intrusions into a child's life than separation from parents' (Little, 2005,
p. 22) and, when such an intrusion is contemplated, it is because all
alternatives have been exhausted.

Foster care

Foster care is probably the single most valuable and most used social
work service for children and families and has been so in its many
forms for many years. An up-to-date working description is that
foster care can include the provision of:

- planned short breaks for a child or young person;
- immediate but temporary care for a child or young person
  with the aim of supporting him or her to return permanently
  to their birth family or to move to a permanent substitute
  family; to support throughcare or aftercare arrangements
  in residential care; or to support him or her in transition to
  independent living;
- specialist care, for example, intensive fostering for young
  people with behavioural problems as an alternative to secure
  care;
- a permanent substitute home for a child who cannot return to
  live with their birth family, by means of a Permanence Order
  or other legal provision. (Scottish Government, 2007, p. 13)

The practice of foster care recognises that the majority of children
and young people normally live in families so practitioners attempt

to ensure that a temporary place in a foster family provides under-standing, care and protection. Given that those children and young people who need to be fostered whether for a weekend, a month or longer, are those who have experienced varying degrees of neglect, the need for good-quality care is vital. Foster care also involves the maintenance of continuity of a child's links with their family and other significant connections in their lives. In the case of contact with birth families, this may be supervised and take place only under certain conditions.

Standards for *private fostering* are covered in the Foster Children (Scotland) Act 1984. Private fostering is where a parent makes an arrangement with someone who is not a close relative, to care for their child. That is a 'private' arrangement. If the child is to stay with the other person for more than twenty-eight days at a time, then there are duties on the parent and the carer, under the 1984 Act, to notify the local authority of the arrangement. The local author-ity then has a duty to check that the arrangements and carers are satisfactory.

All local authorities offer a fostering service and there are a grow-ing number of independent agencies that recruit foster parents and offer foster care. Some such as Barnardo's specialise in finding foster families for children who are severely disabled or for large sibling groups who need to stay together.

Adoption

Adoption is the legal permanent transfer of parental rights to new parents (Scottish Executive, 2002, p. 40). An adoption order is final and cannot be revoked. A child's name is changed to that of their adoptive family (although a first name may be retained), the child's original birth certificate is annotated 'adopted' and an Adoption Order is issued, an abbreviated version of which serves as a new birth certificate.

Adoption law in Scotland was introduced in 1930 with the Adop-tion of Children (Scotland) Act. Prior to this, adoption occurred but it was not legally formalised and sometimes resulted in birth parents taking the children back when the child had reached an age when he or she could work, with little or no recourse for the adoptive parents or child (Ball, 2002, p. 286). The case for the introduction of the Act in 1930 was to legalise the process to 'provide security for the adoptive parents and the children' by transferring completely parental rights and responsibilities to the new parents (ibid.).

There are two main types of adoption:

- where the child is a relative of the adopters, and is not placed by an agency. Such adoptions are often referred to as 'step parent adoptions'. In recent years around half of all adoption applications have consistently been step parent adoptions;
- where the child is placed with the prospective parents by an adoption agency.

All thirty-two local authorities must offer adoption and related services as part of their services for children and adults. Voluntary adoption agencies approved by the Scottish Government and regulated by Social Care and Social Work Improvement Scotland (SCSWIS) can also provide adoption services, three of which assess and approve adoption applications. These are Scottish Adoption and St Andrew's Children's Society based in Edinburgh and St Margaret's Children and Family Care Society in Glasgow. The others provide specialist services, as follows:

- British Association for Adoption & Fostering (BAFF) provides advice, information, training and consultancy services to local authorities and voluntary adoption agencies across Scotland;
- Birthlink's services are for all adults affected by adoption in Scotland and include counselling, tracing, go-between work and post-contact support. It also maintains the Adoption Contact Register for Scotland. (This is a confidential computerised database that puts adopted people and their birth parents, or other birth relatives, in touch when both parties want this to happen);
- Scottish Adoption Advice Service is based in Glasgow and provides post-adoption services to adoptive families and children and young people who have been adopted. Services include advice, counselling, information and help with contacting relatives.

As discussed in Chapter 1, adoption services today have changed from a concentration on the adoption of babies by non-relatives to the adoption — usually from local authority care — of children who have been unable to be looked after by their families of origin. Whether the case be that of the so-called 'relinquished' babies of the 1960s and 1970s or the neglected and rejected children and young people of the 2000s, adoption is a powerful intervention in the life of a child. And it is much more than an event. It is also a life-long process. The life-changing, life-long lasting nature, much emphasised by those who work with adopted adults, is now officially recognised in legislation. For example, reference is now made to the duty 'to safeguard and promote the welfare of the child *throughout the child's life*' (Adoption and Children (Scotland) Act 2007, Section 14(3), emphasis added) and policy now acknowledges 'the lifelong issues for adopted people, adopters and birth parents' (Scottish Government, 2011a).

As to which is the best choice for a child — foster care or adoption — this dilemma has challenged practitioners and families for decades. Often adoption and foster care have gone hand-in-hand with adoption following unsuccessful combinations of temporary foster care and family support, or in the case of 'parallel planning', as discussed in Chapter 1. The introduction of a new legal concept governing the child's position in a family — the Permanence Order (PO) also discussed next — and a strong emphasis on care within the extended family — Kinship Care discussed in Chapter 4 — may see a better settlement of the dilemmas posed by trying to balance the best and long-term interests of the child.

The service context of adoption and fostering
There are 920,000 children under sixteen in Scotland (GRO, 2009). General services for children and young people, such as nurseries, schools and youth provision like clubs, are available to everyone. This book is about the 1% of Scottish children and young people whose families are unable to care for them and who may then need services that will provide temporary, long-term or permanent alternatives to their families. However, it is important to emphasise that any children who do require such services ought to continue to benefit from universal provisions. This is an important ethos that underpins Getting It Right For Every Child (GIRFEC) — see below.

GETTING IT RIGHT FOR EVERY CHILD

The GIRFEC initiative is a central strategy of the Scottish Government's approach to improving outcomes for children in need. Its main philosophy sees the child at the centre surrounded firstly by universal health and education services, then secondly by services tailored to needs and thirdly by services that are compulsorily required in the best interests of the child.

Every child and young person in Scotland is on a journey through life: experiencing rapid development and change as they make the transition from childhood through adolescence and into adulthood. As they progress, some may have temporary difficulties, some may live with challenges that distract them on their journey and some may experience more complex issues. No matter where they live or whatever their needs, children and families should know where they can find help, what support might be available and whether that help is right for them.

GIRFEC's key aspirations for children and young people are for them to be:

- healthy — experiencing the highest standards of physical and mental health, and be supported to make healthy safe choices;
- achieving — receiving support and guidance in their learning, boosting their skills, confidence and self-esteem;
- nurtured — having a nurturing and stimulating place to live and grow;
- active — offered opportunities to take part in a wide range of activities, helping them to build a fulfilling and happy future;
- respected — to be given a voice and involved in the decisions that affect their well-being;
- responsible — taking an active role within their schools and communities;
- included — receiving help and guidance to overcome social, educational, physical and economic inequalities; accepted as full members of the communities in which they live and learn; and above all, to be
- safe — protected from abuse, neglect or harm.

For children, young people and their families, getting it right for every child means they:

- feel confident about the help they are getting;
- understand what is happening and why;
- have been listened to carefully and their wishes have been heard and understood;
- are appropriately involved in discussions and decisions that affect them;
- can rely on appropriate help being available as soon as possible;
- have experienced a more streamlined and co-ordinated response from practitioners.

For practitioners, GIRFEC means:

- putting the child or young person at the centre and developing a shared understanding within and across agencies;

○ using common tools and processes, considering the child or young person as a whole, and promoting closer working where necessary with other practitioners. (Scottish Government, 2007, 2008a)

Assessment for and the provision of substitute family care is the responsibility of local authorities and carried out by social workers. Before the option of substitute family care is considered, families will have received help, and local authorities have a particular duty to provide this to 'children in need' under the terms of the Children (Scotland) Act 1995. The Act is concerned with:

- 'children in need' for whom local authorities have a particular duty to provide services;
- children who may need compulsory measures for their own care and protection and/or on account of their behaviour;
- children who are 'looked after' by local authorities, i.e. children who are being supervised at home as well as away from home; the latter children are often referred to as 'accommodated and looked after' — this category includes children who are in residential care or fostered.

Most children and young people who require compulsory measures of care will have these agreed via the Children's Hearing system (see box), under Section 70 of the Children (Scotland) Act 1995. These children and young people then become 'looked after' by their local authority. The majority are subject to a supervision require-ment naming their parent; some may have a condition of residence naming a friend or relative. When the supervision requirement names a foster carer or residential establishment, children or young people are 'looked after and accommodated'. Some looked after chil-dren and young people become looked after and accommodated on a voluntary basis under Section 25 of the Children (Scotland) Act 1995.

CHILDREN'S HEARINGS

Children's Hearings are panels composed of three lay people who receive referrals from the police, social workers and schools, and less frequently from health services and the child's parents, where there is reasonable cause to believe that a child may require compulsory measures of supervision. Social workers provide reports and these help the Reporter to the Hearing to make a decision as to how to proceed. The Reporter can decide to take no further action, refer the case to the local authority for help or take the case to a Hearing. As this is not a court, the proceedings are not designed to be adversarial. The Hearing may decide to discharge a case, continue for further reports or impose compulsory measures of supervision. This last disposal could mean that the child remains on supervision at home or within the wider family or enters foster or residential care. Children thus become 'looked after and accommodated' and the ultimate responsibility for overseeing their welfare is that of the local authority. In the case of children who are looked after and accommodated and for whom adoption is deemed the best solution for their long-term care, a Hearing must also look at and approve the plan.

Although originally established to engage with problems of juvenile delinquency and law-breaking, over the past twenty years the Hearings have seen a rise in numbers of children being referred because of welfare neglect and abuse, to the extent that the latter referrals now outnumber those that are made because of concerns over behaviour. In 2009/10, 42,532 children in Scotland were referred to the Children's Reporter, of whom 35,735 were referred on non-offence (care and protection) grounds and 10,012 on offence grounds. (SCRA, 2010)

'Looked after and accommodated'

Children who are 'looked after and accommodated' in Scotland are children and young people living in foster care or residential units, though an increasing number are being placed with relatives or friends. They are usually placed there as a result of a voluntary agreement between the family and a local authority, by a supervision requirement from a Children's Hearing or following an emergency child protection order. Children may be looked after (but not 'accommodated') at home under the terms of Children's Hearing supervision order. About 1.1% of Scotland's children are 'looked after' (SWIA, 2006).

Being 'looked after and accommodated' confers a legal status on the child concerned and, whilst parental rights are retained, this obliges the local authority to oversee and secure, if necessary, the child's care and protection. The change of terminology from reception or coming into, or being in 'care' to 'looked after and accommodated' signalled an effort to shift from a description that evoked a more authoritarian local authority intervention to one that emphasised partnership with parents in the process of providing alternative care for a child. (Popular parlance, however, has tended to stick with 'care', with 'looked after and accommodated' shortened to LAAC, as in 'an LAAC child', which is more generally used for finance and administration purposes.)

At 31 July 2010 there were 15,892 children looked after by local authorities, an increase of 4% since 2009. The number of children looked after has increased every year since 2001 and is at its highest since 1982:

- 39% of children looked after were at home with parents and 20% were looked after by friends or relatives;
- 30% were looked after by foster carers;
- 9% were in residential accommodation. (Scottish Government, 2011b)

The overwhelming majority of children are looked after for care and protection reasons and that proportion, compared to other reasons such as offending, is increasing annually. Children and young people may be looked after for short or long periods; some are at home, some return home, some may be adopted and some remain looked after for many years until they reach adulthood. Some children experience all of these processes.

There are many reasons why children become looked after:

- some children have experienced neglect;
- some children have experienced mental, physical or emotional abuse;
- some parents are unable to look after their children because of their own substance misuse;
- some young people need time out from their birth family while support is provided to try to rebuild family relationships or their ability to function;
- some children have complex disabilities and need to be placed in specialist residential schools;
- some children, because of their behaviour, will have become involved in the youth criminal justice system.

Local authorities have a duty to provide advice and support to looked after young people up to age nineteen, and the power to do so up to age twenty-one. They are required to make sure that when young people leave care[1] they are equipped with the necessary life skills and receive adequate financial and other support at what is a difficult time for all young people. Getting this package of support right is crucial to improving outcomes for care leavers to make sure they have the stability and support they require to fulfil their potential educationally and to develop the life skills to enable them to make a successful transition to independent living. Sections 29 and 30 of the Children (Scotland) Act 1995 set out local authorities' responsibilities to care leavers. As we will see, over the past two decades there has been a rising concern about the poor preparation and support offered to young people leaving local authority care (see, for example, SWIA, 2006).

The service context of adoption and fostering would not be complete without a note regarding the more classic form of adoption and its place in local authority services. The adoption of infants who have not been in local authority care is often called 'stranger' adoptions and means adoption by non-relatives as distinct from adoption within the family such as by step-parents, The adoption of infants by non-relatives continues and there were sixty-three such adoptions of children under two in 2009. Local authorities are required to undertake a full assessment and approval of all those who wish to adopt. They are also required to provide post-adoption support to all adopted children and their adoptive families and this will be looked at in greater depth in Chapter 2. In relation to adopted adults, it should be noted that, whilst not every adopted adult needs a service, a rough estimate based on the number of Scottish adoptions of people who are now over eighteen years old suggests that there are some 85,000 adopted adults in Scotland. The degree to which other adults affected by adoption — for example, birth parents and other birth relatives — receive support has been somewhat neglected or left to the voluntary sector. New legislation indicates that this may be redressed and is further discussed in Chapter 5.

Because this book is primarily for practitioners and those who wish to become so, the following extract from *These Are Our Bairns* is

---

1 See p. xx about the popular use of the term 'care' — leave 'having been accommodated' doesn't have the same ring nor does it convey the reality, especially at such a crucial point.

chosen as a signpost to the values and practice principles that underpin the following chapters. It is addressed to social workers:

You will want to:

- have the same aspirations, hopes and expectations which all good parents have for their own children;
- be the professional who holds together the life story of the child or young person and makes sure that life events which are important do not get lost but are recognised and stored;
- be confident that the child or young person is safe, healthy, active, nurtured, achieving, respected and responsible, and included;
- make sure that wherever the child or young person lives they feel they belong, are secure and that they can grow in confidence as their developing needs continue to be met;
- make sure that a child or young person is only moved if it is in her/his best interests and the transition is carefully planned, managed and explained to the child or young person;
- make sure the child or young person is truly involved in decisions which affect them and that they get the support and opportunity to state their views which are listened to and taken seriously;
- expect the best from all services so they can help the child or young person to reach their full potential and that there is someone who advocates for them in the same way as good parents do;
- make sure that all the child or young person's achievements are recognised and the ones most important to the young person are remembered and recorded;
- make sure that the child or young person's care plan takes full account of their educational needs and identifies how adults with different roles can help their achievement in school;

- encourage and support the young person to consider post-sixteen education, training or employment;
- make sure the child or young person has the opportunity to have new experiences, for example, staying overnight with a friend or going on a school journey and to try out new skills such as sport, music, drama, arts and culture;
- make sure that the child or young person is part of their local community and can use local universal services without discrimination. Where there are institutional barriers you will be confident in approaching the relevant agencies to tackle these;
- understand the strengths and difficulties of the child or young person's family relationships and recognise family members who are important to them and support professionals in recognising and helping these relationships to be positive;
- encourage the child or young person to make and keep friends;
- encourage young people to continue to be looked after until they are eighteen, if that is in their best interests. They should be ready to live independently and should not move into independence as a reaction to placement breakdown;
- recognise that taking risks is part of growing up and to support carers of the child or young person to let them take reasonable risks at age-appropriate stages;
- help the child or young person negotiate each life transition and that a child or young person looked after away from home does not miss out on what might be taken for granted by good parents: for example, remembering the age they started to walk; joined local youth groups; took part in religious festivals or family events when relatives gather and family history is updated and exchanged. (Scottish Government, 2008b, p. 33)

This introduction has outlined the significant features of adoption and fostering and the service context of these two vital services for children and families. It is hoped that the following chapters will not only inform but also inspire the best possible practice.

CHAPTER 1

Adoption & Fostering in Scotland: Yesterday and Today

This chapter is concerned with main changes and trends in adoption and fostering. It will provide an overview of developments that have shaped the face of today's practice and will influence tomorrow's services. The discussion will include the decline of 'stranger' adoptions, important legislative initiatives such as the Adoption and Children (Scotland) Act 2007 and the growth in our understanding of what it means to be a child in care.

Because this book is not a history of adoption and fostering in Scotland, this chapter concentrates on what we have learnt in more recent years. Much of our knowledge has emanated from elsewhere in the UK and where appropriate this will be encompassed. The research for this chapter has also studied all research reviews, reports and other publications of particular Scottish relevance covering the past twenty years. This is a period that spans the introduction of the Children (Scotland) Act 1995 and the devolution of responsibility for social services in 1999.

Like most countries, Scotland has a history and tradition of caring for others' children. The practice of 'boarding out' children who could not, for whatever reason but mostly poverty, live in their family of origin is as old as families and caring themselves. Boarded-out arrangements took place between people and sometimes were overseen by local worthies such as a GP or a minister of the church. Boarding out could be for months — sometimes specifically timed to coincide with helping with harvests or it could be for years and look toward an apprenticeship (for a boy). Other instances would involve family members who were distant (in both senses of the word) or placing the child with a childless person or couple who didn't have to worry about the cost of an extra mouth to feed. In nearly all cases the family of origin had some knowledge of the whereabouts of the child. Towards the end of the nineteenth century, with the rise of child welfare organisations and formal interventions in family life, a more official structure developed imbued by notions of child rescue involving Child Shelters and Children's Homes to which children were removed, often never to see their family again. For those interested in this period prior to emergence of the adoption and fostering legislation of the twentieth century, Abrams' *The Orphan Country* (1998) is a rich source and Ball (2002) provides a brief but helpful background to the first Scottish adoption legislation in 1930 — the Adoption of Children (Scotland) Act.

Apart from the milestone of the Social Work (Scotland) Act 1968, which led to the establishment of the Children's Hearings system, Scottish adoption and fostering practice has not departed much from that of the rest of the UK except for a few notable differences such as Scottish adopted people always having had the right of access to their original birth certificate. This remains relatively true today. However, as we will see, there have been a number of recent developments, principal of which has been the Scottish Adoption Policy Review launched by the then new Scottish Executive in 2000. These initiatives have begun to craft a specifically Scottish adoption and fostering service.

Fostering

What has shaped contemporary adoption and fostering? Little begins his review of fostering research with a crucial reminder:

> Looked after children come from economically poor families. By now, this hardly needs to be said; Sinclair uses one sentence to state the obvious. What cannot be said, because the research is not set up to show it, is that most people working in or commentating on the care system would not let their own children anywhere near it. (Little, 2005, p. 12)

Whilst noting that fashions come and go and being struck by how little radical change appears to have taken place over the twenty years since 1985, Little suggests that a 'big' change has been the rise of foster care and the decline of residential care as an option for children who have been maltreated. The Scottish figures bear this out (see Table 1.1).

Table 1.1: Changing numbers of children in foster care and residential care since 1976 (SWIA, 2006)

	1976	1987	1997	2007	2010
In residential care	6,242	2,784	1,960	1,661	1,480
With foster carers or prospective adoptive parents	3,763	2,750	2,635	4,275	4,996

This trend has continued and at the beginning of the 2000s foster care was accurately described as the 'workhorse of the child care system (Kelly and Gilligan, 2000, p. 9). It is now the most common option for looked after children, with temporary foster care being the most commonly used type of foster care (SCIE, 2004b).

The other 'big change' is that the nature of foster care has altered. According to Hill, foster care has been given an expanded role to provide not only daily care, but also parental support, life story or therapeutic help to emotionally damaged children and preparation for moving back home or on to adoption (Hill, 2002c, p. 19). This increase in the expectations of foster care is a result of the fact that foster care has developed as the placement of choice for 'some young people who were formerly thought to require residential care and who tend to be more testing in their behaviour' (Hill, 2002b, p. 13). A second element that has altered the nature of fostering has been the emphasis in the Children Acts of 1989 (England and Wales) and 1995 (Scotland) on the importance of supporting children in their families wherever possible. Such efforts have meant that the threshold for being cared for outwith the family is higher and, for a child who needs such care, their needs are not only greater but also compounded by failed attempts at family re-integration. Such children will also remain in care longer and can be regarded as 'growing up in care' for years and sometimes until adulthood (Bullock et al., 2006). These changes in the nature of and demands on foster care constitute the second 'big' change in foster care.

There are a variety of other themes and demands on foster care that have emerged over the past twenty years.

Foster care and contact

During the 1980s and 1990s, the importance of contact between children in care and their birth parents emerged, stressing the value to the child of maintaining the connection with the birth family. Contact could promote continuity and might possible assist in reunification. It also could maintain sibling links and connections with extended birth family members such as grandparents. The research also pointed to the neglect or discouragement of these connections by social workers expressed in, for example, the lack of support offered to birth family members to keep up contact once the child had come into care (Moyers *et al.*, 2006). And despite expressions of doubt about what may be portrayed as the universal benefit and applicability of contact 'regardless of family circumstances and relationships' (Quinton *et al.*, 1997, p. 411), the benefit and promotion of contact between a child in care and their birth family have now become a principle and presumption in legislation and policy (Triselitotis, 2010).

CONTACT DEFINED

DIRECT CONTACT means meetings between the child/young person and birth family members and/or significant others, and includes phone calls, texting, emails and other forms of electronic communication such as Facebook.

INDIRECT CONTACT means letters and cards from members of the birth family and significant others, usually through a third party.

Contact is a key issue for children and they often have ambivalent feelings, both wanting it but feeling distressed at the same time. They often desire more contact with fathers and other family members, such as grandmothers and siblings, even if they are happy in their placement and do not want to return home. Parents also have these ambivalent feelings. Many desperately miss their children, want to have contact and find the experience distressing.

Current practice assumes a strong principle, supported by legislation, that contact is generally beneficial and should be promoted, unless it is not in the child's best interests. Decisions need to be made on the different aspects of contact: for example, contact with family members. Contact must always be 'fine tuned', assessing and taking into account any risks. (SCIE, 2004b)

Generally, foster carers are in the day-to-day 'front line' in managing and supporting contact arrangements (SCIE, 2004b), and challenges such as contact are a contributory factor in the process of recasting and professionalisation of foster care.

The professionalisation of fostering

No longer are carers seen merely as well-intentioned volunteers providing for young, unproblematic, deprived children. The task and expectations are greater and research findings, such as these, have an important role in raising standards and providing improved experiences for children, families and carers alike. (Berridge, 2005, p. 8)

The recognition of such challenges for foster carers is embodied in the move away from the provision of an allowance to the payment of salaries and fees that recognise the increase in depth of need, and the skills required to meet this, and the development of specialist foster carers — specifically recruited, trained and supported — who provide care for children with special needs such as learning disabilities or for those possibly suffering from the effects of serious maltreatment. A Social Work Inspection Agency (SWIA) report into the care and protection of children in Eilean Siar concludes:

The placement of sexually abused children in foster homes requires intensive support and help for the family in understanding the issues the child may bring to them ... Foster carers should have appropriate initial and ongoing training and support to help them to understand and manage the children they are caring for and sustain their own family. (SWIA, 2005, p. 66)

In 1996, Fife was one of the first authorities to pay all its foster carers a professional fee as well as an allowance (Hill, 2002d, p. 284). Preparation training before approval as a foster carer is now universal and in-service training has become an embedded and integral part of the overall service (SCIE, 2004b). In recognition of the complexities of delivering good-quality foster care, the Scottish Government has acknowledged that foster carers ought to be seen as co-professionals alongside social workers and consequently paid and resourced as such (Scottish Government, 2007). It remains to be seen whether such aspirations will be translated into changed practice on the ground. In England and Wales, it was expected that the Children Act 1989 would herald a more collegiate approach between social workers and foster carers; however, a study revealed that there was little evidence of this:

> One of the most notable differences in the interview content was the lack of autonomy felt by the foster carers. Carers complained bitterly about their inability to take or influence decisions and the bureaucracy to which they were subjected. Some had to ask permission to get the child's hair cut or had to get approval for babysitters or had no authority to give permissions for school trips or other educational activities. Sleep-overs, a very important part of children's lives, were impossible to arrange as SSDs [Social Service Departments] needed weeks to make decisions and do police checks. Consequently, carers were faced with the dilemma of either denying the young person the opportunity to lead a 'normal life' or lying to social services. (Selwyn and Quinton, 2004, p. 13)

This is echoed in the same Scottish Government report that called for the recognition of foster carers as co-professionals: 'Foster carer responses include calls for the professionalisation of their role. Associated with this were comments that they do not feel their opinions and experience are valued by professional staff' (Scottish Government, 2007, p. 44). It seems, therefore, that the professionalisation of foster care, although an official aspiration, remains patchy and is yet to be a greater reality on the ground.

Concern over placement moves
The number of times a child moves during their period in care has been a matter of concern for many years and attention to this has been growing since the beginning of the 2000s. Ward and Skuse

(2001) found that, in the first year of being fostered, many children moved placements at least once, twice or even three times. 'Planned move' was given as the reason for not only the first move but also the second and third moves as well. Many children have periods at home interspersed with periods in care, often not in the same placement. This means that, in effect, the child is in long-term foster care, which results in a great deal of uncertainty and generally poor outcomes (SCIE, 2004b). In Scotland, children looked after away from home have an average 3.07 placement moves in each period 'in care' (Scottish Executive, 2002). During the Scottish Adoption Policy Review process, young people who were or had been in foster care added their voices to the need for greater placement stability (Scottish Executive, 2005). A recent Who Cares? Scotland survey has reaffirmed that placement moves remain a matter of concern for children in care (Who Cares? Scotland, 2010).

Attention to service users' voices

Fostering and adoption encompass many categories of service users including, obviously, children. However, within the gender-neutral terms of 'foster parents', 'birth parents' and 'adoptive parents', the voices of fathers have tended not to be heard though there is growing acknowledgement of the separate experiences (and contributions) of men (see, for example, Clapton, 2003a on birth fathers; Wilson *et al.*, 2007 on foster fathers; and Feast *et al.*, 2011 on adoptive fathers). As regards children, a success story is that their voices are now routinely included in many research studies and official publications — an example of this is the embedding of children's views in the Scottish Adoption Policy review process. 'Who Cares? Scotland' has come to play a major role in gathering and articulating the voices and experiences of people in foster care (Who Cares? Scotland, 2009).

The degree to which children's voices are heard and acted upon is another matter. Leeson's work with young people in care has charted the development of feelings of helplessness, low self-esteem and poor confidence that have followed the lack of opportunities for young people to make decisions about their own lives (Leeson, 2007, p. 268). She concludes:

Although policy-makers acknowledge this (the dangers and unfairness of ignoring children) and are making steps to ensure children in care meaningfully participate in decision-making about their care (Department for Education and Skills, 2006), research shows there is a long way to go (Parker, 2006), especially for the younger child. (Leeson, 2007, p. 276)

A FOSTER CARER SPEAKS[1]

'Myself, my husband and our three children started fostering ten years ago.

'We saw and continue to see our role as carers as one which requires a professional approach, a setting of standards, contributing to a team, undertaking our tasks and responsibilities with the seriousness and diligence that the lives of these children and young people merited.

'I am regulated, monitored, assessed and standardised.

'I write reports, attend meetings, submit forms, keep my paperwork in order, record my days, attend training, as well as wipe noses and bottoms, sing songs and read stories, and act as mother, teacher, taxi driver, counsellor, therapist, nurse, spiritual advisor, confidante, rule giver, cook, nutritionist, careers advisor, pillow, whipping boy, moderator, IT consultant, advocate, bank manager, librarian, encyclopaedia, legal advisor, and just be there.' (Scottish Government, 2007, p. 15)

Growth of interest in outcomes for looked after children
In the last twenty-five years there has been a burgeoning of literature on the health, education and other outcomes for children who have been in care (Jackson, 2007). Stein's research review suggests that there are different outcomes for three categories of young people leaving care. These are those who are 'moving on', those who are 'surviving' and those becoming 'victims'. Required for the latter are:

more comprehensive responses across their life course: (1) early intervention and family support; (2) providing better-quality care to compensate them for their damaging pre-care experiences through stability and continuity, as well as assistance to overcome educational deficits; (3) providing opportunities for more gradual transitions from care that

---

1 This is the first of a series of voices from adoption and fostering service users that will run throughout the book.

are more akin to normative transitions; and (4) providing ongoing support to those young people who need it, especially those young people with mental health problems and complex needs. (Stein, 2006, p. 278)

These are the challenges that need to be met by the GIRFEC initiative and the adoption and fostering legislative and policy reforms.

Leaving care
This discussion of changes in conceptions of fostering would not be complete without some reference to what happens after young people leave care. Little suggests:

> Potentially the most significant change has been the lengthening of the period of 'care' into early adulthood. The state has come to recognise that parental obligations do not stop at the child's 16th or 18th birthday. Children fostered in adolescence now have a right for support until their 21st birthday. This is still an arbitrary cut-off point that rarely reflects the needs of young people or the obligations felt by foster parents, but it is an improvement on the previous situation all the same. (Little, 2005, p.15)

The experiences, circumstances and opportunities of young people who leave care, as for a number of other 'recognitions' that are contained in this overview of developments remain a matter of concern. At the end of the 2000s, an important investigation from the Scottish Commissioner for Children and Young People found:

> Time and again, young people and workers told us about a strong culture that assumed 16 was the age at which young people should leave care. This was reinforced by language about 'moving on' introduced before the young person was 16 and by practices such as filling out housing applications forms soon after their 16th birthdays. (Scottish Commissioner for Children and Young People, 2008, p. 9)

The commissioner found that the consequences of leaving care aged sixteen or seventeen, when young people are not ready to face the challenges this presents, include 'getting into rent arrears, becoming involved with drugs/alcohol, difficulties with neighbours, threat of eviction which sometimes leads to homelessness, and difficulties sustaining education' (Scottish Commissioner for Children and Young People, 2008, p. 27).

Adoption

There were 455 adoptions in Scotland in 2009. Longer-term trends show an overall decline. The number of adoptions peaked in 1946 and 1969 at 2,298 and 2,268, respectively. Over the long term the age of children being adopted has increased: 14% of children who were adopted in 2009 were under two, compared to 69% in 1962. Not all of this number will have been adopted from care.

In recent years, around 1% of all looked after children in Scotland were placed for adoption. While the scale of adoption activity is considerably smaller than fostering, adoption agencies have a significant role in providing alternative, secure family placements for looked after children who cannot return to the family they were born into. In 2007, a Care Commission report indicated that, after allowing for step-parent adoptions and children adopted from other countries, 184 children were placed with prospective adopters (Scottish Commission for the Regulation of Care, 2007, p. 38). This figure does not include the small number of infants not in care that had been placed for adoption with non-relatives and, therefore, the numbers of children being adopted from care may be fewer than 150 that year (see Table 1.2).

Table 1.2: Adoptions in Scotland 1930–2009 (GRO, 2009)

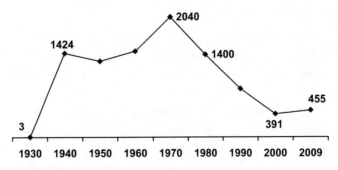

The statistics highlight the changing characteristics of adoption in Scotland. Whereas traditionally a typical adoption was a single mother unable to keep her child, changing attitudes have meant that this rarely occurs now. The decline in the number of infant adoptions can be explained by two main factors:

- the availability of contraception and abortion, which led to a decreased number of 'unwanted births';
- the rise of a greater acceptance of children born outside marriage, i.e. the stigma of illegitimacy and societal disapproval began to decline.

Whilst the number of children placed for adoption by adoption agencies has fallen, the levels of difficulty and disability of the children that are placed have grown considerably. Services that were originally designed to find adoptive placements for healthy babies have changed and developed into finding homes for some of the most disadvantaged children in Scotland (Scottish Executive, 2002): for example, children entering care now are more likely to have been affected by their parents' misuse of drugs and alcohol. Many children have been subject to harm (physical, sexual or emotional) and/or neglect.

In England, between 2004 and 2007, 74% of the children adopted from the care system had been abused or neglected prior to entering the care system (DCSF, 2007). Furthermore, many of these children experience moves within the care system and delays in the adoption process (Ball, 2002, p. 9). This leads to increased difficulties in adoption placements for the children and their adoptive parents. So, whilst there are still babies adopted to non-relatives, the children that are adopted today are those who will have known their birth parents and other birth relatives such as grandparents or other siblings — and may hold feelings, some mixed, for these people.

What now follows is a broad-brush picture of the major issues that have emerged in the twenty-three years since the last major adoption legislation of 1978. Some of these will be returned to in depth.

The development of openness and contact in adoption

Just as contact between children and birth family members is an increasing feature of practice and policy in foster care, equally contact in adoption has become a central principle in adoption planning and support. Post-adoption contact arrangements have been rare and are not encouraged in law. However, a mixture of social and practice developments have ensured that contact after adoption is now a feature of the majority of adoptions from care. Changes that have brought this about include the increase in numbers of children who will have had contact with their parents and have developed relationships with other members of their birth families such as siblings (PIU, 2000); an appreciation of the unresolved grief experienced by birth mothers and the need for information about their child's continued well-being (Charlton *et al.*, 1998); and mounting evidence that the previous 'clean break' philosophy of adoption, in which ties and associations with family of origin were discouraged, was detrimental to the well-being and identity needs of adopted people (Howe and Feast, 2000).

In the mid-1990s, a UK judge summed up the case for contact in a child's interests:

> In short, even when the Section 31 criteria are satisfied, contact may well be of singular importance to the long-term welfare of the child: first, in giving the child the security of knowing that his parents love him and are interested in his welfare; secondly, by avoiding any damaging sense of loss to the child in seeing himself abandoned by his parents; thirdly, by enabling the child to commit himself to the substitute family with the seal of approval of the natural parents; and, fourthly, by giving the child the necessary sense of family and personal identity. Contact, if maintained, is capable of reinforcing and increasing the chances of success of a permanent placement, whether on a long-term fostering basis or by adoption. (Judgement of Simon Brown LJ, quoted in Brammer, 2009, p. 331)

In 2002 the Scottish Government investigation into adoption policy and practice found that:

> contact between children and young people who are adopted and those who were important to them prior to their adoption is increasingly maintained, either directly or indirectly. (Scottish Executive, 2002)

More recently a leading UK researcher noted: 'a general move towards thinking about "when", "why" and "how" contact might work or not work, as opposed to "if" contact works' (Neil, 2009, p. 8). Thus practice is constantly being developed and refined (Sellick, 2007). In the USA, McRoy (1991) identifies some thirty types of contact in adoption ranging from complete openness, where, for example, the birth parent(s) is known to and in regular face-to-face contact with the adoptive family and child, to the more common forms (in the UK) of exchanged information updates between the adoptive parents and one or more members of the birth family: for example, a sibling, grandparent or birth parent. Neil notes that: 'in the majority of cases, contact is likely to take the form of mediated written exchanges, as opposed to face-to-face meetings' (Neil, 2009, p. 8). Today, contact arrangements are better seen as not fixed, either in time or type and 'mutually developmental' (Grotevant and McRoy, 1998).

Such moves towards greater contact in adoption sit within wider changes of attitude in favour of more openness in adoption, which apply to more than arrangements for contact after adoption. Openness in adoption may cover the opportunity for birth parents and prospective adoptive parents to meet with each other during adoption planning. It also refers to the practice of greater access to adoption records (Clapton, 2008). It should be noted that in Scotland the Adoption of Children Act 1930, allowed adopted adults the right to their original birth certificate (this was introduced only in 1976 in the rest of the UK).

The *Guidance* on the Adoption and Children (Scotland) Act 2007 contains an acknowledgement of the trend to greater access to case records:

> For the adopted person returning, there is often a need to fill in gaps in their knowledge both of their birth family and of themselves as young children. Adoption agency procedures should be clear about both expectations of the process for gathering and keeping the information about a child which will be vital for them as an adult. (Scottish Government, 2011a)

On the wider issue of greater transparency in adoption planning, the recent legislative and policy initiatives indicate an awareness of the importance of birth parent involvement. On this front there is much to do. In 2004, the Social Care Institute for Excellence (SCIE) notes:

> A 2003 study found that 50 per cent of care plans, where children were to be fostered permanently did not specify the parents' role in decision-making. In 75 per cent of cases the care plans did not say how disagreements should be resolved, despite the fact that parental responsibility remained shared between the birth parents and local authority. (SCIE, 2004b, p. 84)

Permanence and permanency planning

Hill posits:

> In the last 25 years, the most vibrant approach to services for looked after children has been that of permanency planning ... Permanency planning has emphasised efforts to keep children's stays in state care as short as possible. (Hill, 2002c, p. 19)

Permanency planning developed following research that pointed to children 'drifting' in care because of a lack of proper planning for their future (Rowe and Lambert, 1973). The underlying rationale of the concept of permanency planning is that when children cannot be protected within their family and are removed from home, often the best outcome is effective intervention that improves their parents' skills or capacity to care for them and enables them to return home. If this is not possible, other permanent care arrangements should be determined as soon as possible. Permanent options generally include: preventing unnecessary placements through family preservation; return home; long-term or permanent foster care or care by relatives; and adoption (Thoburn, 2003). An official approach has emphasised family support: 'Permanence can be achieved in a number of ways: for example, by working with the child's family to enable the child to return home; by care by other relatives; or by long-term foster care' (Department of Health, Lord Chancellor's Department and Home Office, 1992). However, it has since been noted that in practice 'the emphasis of permanency planning has tended to be on finding permanent substitute families for children rather than on planned work to return them home' (Biehal, 2007, p. 809).

THE SCOTTISH ADOPTION POLICY REVIEW ON THE IMPORTANCE OF PERMANENCE

For children, a sense of belonging — of being cared for and cared about — is fundamental to their healthy emotional and physical development. However, a sense of belonging — for example, being part of a family — is not something that can be established by telling a child that they are now part of a new family, or because they are the subject of a particular legal order. The feeling of permanence comes from the actions and behaviour of those adults who care for the child. For most children their world is what they experience on a day-by-day basis. Daily care routines, familiar meals on set days, planning for holidays, celebrating birthdays all help a child develop both a sense of self-esteem and well-being in the present, and a sense of hope and optimism for the future. It is vital therefore that the adult(s) who are parenting a child on a day-to-day basis are also able to plan for a child, be it for next week, next month, next birthday or the next holiday. The capacity of adults to offer children this continuity and predictability can be impaired by their own personal circumstances, such as drug or alcohol misuse or mental health problems. For those who care for children within public care, there is the added dimension of sharing decision-making with a range of other people, which can lead to differences in view and delays in taking action, which in turn impacts on children who need predictability and consistency. A number of factors can provoke huge anxiety and uncertainty amongst children in public care:

- how long they might live in their current home?
- who will buy them birthday presents?
- will they be going back to the same school in August?
- why are different adults coming to talk to them and their carers?
- why can't they go to sleepover at their friends?
- why do their carers sometimes look anxious, or talk about what will happen at the next meeting, or refer to 'your next family'?

This profound sense of unpredictability and uncertainty is not reduced by sharing information about future plans with the child or by allowing the child to participate in decision-making. Having your life planned and scrutinised by a wide range of adults is not a normal experience. Children do not want to be different from their peers in this as in other areas of life. The best solution is therefore for children to be brought up within family situations in which the adults can give children clear messages that they both belong and will continue to be part of that family, and that known and trusted parents are 'in charge'. (Scottish Executive, 2005, pp. 7–8)

Rise of concurrent planning

If permanency planning as a concept was the theory, then concurrent planning could be termed the practice. Concurrent planning as an approach to permanent placement of young children developed in the early 1980s in the USA. Faced with the problems of drift and delay noted above, and children becoming 'hard to place' or 'stuck' in the child care system, the idea of concurrent planning was to speed the placement of children aged under eight into permanent families, either by a return to the birth family or by adoption into a new family. The birth family is supported in addressing the reasons for the child's removal at the same time as the child was placed with a family jointly approved as both foster carers and adopters, who would then go on to adopt the child if rehabilitation of the birth parents failed. The work with birth parents is time limited. In what has become known in the UK as 'twin tracking' or 'parallel planning', and good practice to speed decision-making, this approach requires the assessment of the birth parents, the extended family and the development of a care plan for placement outside the family to be considered simultaneously (Marsh and Thoburn, 2002). The aim is to avoid the time-lags associated with sequential planning by assessing the likelihood of a return home when the child first enters out-of-home care. When the prognosis for a return is poor, work is begun on a permanency plan at the same time as continuing family support that seeks a return of the child.

Concerns have been raised that concurrent planning undermines efforts to return the child to their family, particularly when agencies are not adequately resourced to provide comprehensive or intensive services to birth families (D'Andrade et al., 2006).

Contested adoptions

As the proportion of adoptions in which an infant was relinquished by request fell and the number of adoptions from care rose, so did the numbers of contested adoptions rise. By the end of the 1990s a review for the Department of Health noted that high proportions of adoptions were being contested (Department of Health, 1999). Such litigation is distressing and according to one leading adoption agency:

This work is becoming increasingly complex as the population of birth parents/relatives requiring a service shifts from relinquishing birth parents to contested adoptions where parents/relatives may have complex needs through drug/alcohol use, mental health issues and learning difficulties. (Scottish Adoption, 2006)

Adoption: Better Choices for Our Children called for court procedures to:

be streamlined and dedicated adoption centres introduced, where sheriffs with appropriate experience in family work and active case management can focus on the main issues. This would shorten the length of time that most cases take, and would help to reduce the level of distress typically experienced in contested adoptions. (Scottish Executive, 2005, p. 5).

Time will tell whether the recent legislation and guidance ensure that all parties involved are supported so that the right decisions can be made.

Support for adoptive families

In the days of 'stranger' adoption of babies, after an adoption had taken place, adoptive families would receive a visit or two from the social worker, and then be left to get on with things. Even in these cases, some families came under pressure and were in need of specialist post-adoption support. With the different needs of children being adopted from care today, it has become more and more recognised that post-adoption services need to be in place as a matter of routine. In its written evidence given to the Scottish Parliament during the passage of the 2007 Adoption and Children (Scotland) Act, Edinburgh City Council notes the extensive dissatisfaction of the current post-adoption support services by adopted persons, adopters and birth families:

In particular, there are increasing and usually justified demands from adopters for therapeutic services for their children, for support with the practicalities and emotional impact of contact arrangements and for respite services.

Local authorities, or the voluntary agencies with which they have service level agreements, are currently very over-stretched trying to meet existing demand. (City of Edin-burgh Council, 2006)

The 2007 legislation and subsequent regulations and guidance acknowledge these demands and set out a framework to meet them. Adoption support services are now better defined than hitherto the case in previous legislation and policy. Specific support includes:

- services to meet the therapeutic needs of adopted children;
- assistance to adopters such as training to meet special needs and respite care;
- mediation and other services if there is a disruption in an adoption placement, or risk of one. (Scottish Government, 2011a)

The challenges facing adoptive families will be revisited in the next two chapters.

Life-long nature of adoption
Since the 1980s, adoption support agencies, birth parent organisa-tions, adopted people and research studies have pointed out that adoption is not a single event but a life-long process and experience that involves many parties both whilst the child is growing and after the child comes of age. In the words of practice guidance published by the Department for Children, Schools and Families (DCSF):

Adoption is more than a one-off event. It is an evolving life-long process for all those involved — adopted adults, and birth and adoptive relatives. The fundamental issues raised by adoption may reverberate and resurface at differ-ent times and stages in an individual's life. (DCSF, 2008)

In many places the Scottish adoption legislation and policy initia-tives indicate a relatively new-found position that appreciates that adoption is a life-long process. The 2007 Act, for example, draws attention to: 'the likely effect on the child, throughout the child's life, of the making of an adoption order' (Adoption and Children (Scotland) Act 2007, Part 1, Chapter 2 (14)).

Support for adopted adults, birth parents and birth relatives
Closely connected to the acknowledgement of the life-long nature
of adoption has come the appreciation of the need for services to
adults affected by adoption (Feast, 2010). This together with the rise
of openness in adoption, especially regarding access to records, and
a growing demand from birth parents and other birth relatives for
support services has resulted in a burgeoning of interest and activity
in tracing, mediation and contact between adult adopted people and
birth family members. (This will be discussed in depth in Chapter
5.) However, over the past twenty-five years, interest in and contact between adopted adults and their birth family members have
become common features for those who provide adoption services.
There is now a wide range of publications on the subject: official
(DCSF, 2008), research based (Triseliotis *et al.*, 2005) and anec-
dotal (Adie, 2005). This is aimed at everyone involved, although
many works concentrate on the adopted person's experiences, less
so that of birth parents, and much less so from the perspective of
adoptive parents of an adopted adult who sets out to contact their
birth family.

Reflecting this upsurge in interest and demands on services, the
Adoption and Children (Scotland) Act 2007 has made material
changes to adoption support requirements: for example, these now
include 'assistance, including mediation, in arrangements for contact between adopted children and their birth parents, siblings and
other relatives (Scottish Government, 2011a).

The background document that fed into the 2007 Act went further:

> The Group recommends that there should be a support ser-
> vice for tracing and accessing information as a distinct part
> of the overall adoption support system. This service should
> include the provision of intermediary services for birth par-
> ents and other birth family members and assistance to other
> relatives of adopted people, such as their spouses, children
> or adoptive parents, particularly when the adopted person
> has died or otherwise cannot exercise rights to informa-
> tion. At present, there is disparity in the information and
> services provided around Scotland and a system prescribed

by regulation would provide greater consistency. (Scottish Executive, 2005, p. 104)

Regulations and guidance that have emerged since the Act's assent have not been as precise as this so it remains to be seen whether policy will catch up with the range of imaginative services available to adults in adoption (albeit, mostly operated by the non-statutory agencies such as Birthlink and the Scottish Adoption Advice Service).

Disruption

As the needs of children who are adopted have become more complex, so an interest has grown in what is described as 'adoption disruption'. The Care Commission defines adoption disruption as 'a breakdown leading to the young person no longer living with the adopters' (Scottish Commission for the Regulation of Care, 2007, p. 4). According to the Care Commission, a total of 6.2% of children placed for adoption experienced disruption in 2005–6 (ibid., p. 38). The Commission's definition of disruption tends to mask the fact that a child or young person whose adoption has failed is essentially one whose relationship with their (new) parents may be over. And that child may very well return to the care system. Concern has grown because the collection of data has been hampered by the lack of an agreed definition: for example, what length of time should pass before it is agreed that an adoption has broken down?

The Prime Minister's review of adoption in England and Wales summarised a number of key research studies and found disruption rates for children placed for adoption at seven or eight years old were 20% with this rate increasing with the age of child to as much as 50% of adoptions (with a dip to 40% breakdown in adoptions of children in their late teens). The more positive message was that there was a clear correlation between the younger children and lower chances of disruption (PIU, 2000). Perhaps with the Scottish Adoption Act's introduction of Permanence Orders, such distressing breakdowns and disruptions will be minimised.

Adoption Act 2007

This brings us to the Adoption and Children (Scotland) Act 2007. Although the practice changes heralded by the Act will be discussed more fully in the next chapters, it would not be proper to finish this chapter reviewing developments without reference to the most major piece of adoption legislation and policy for nearly thirty years. The Act can be seen as legislation catching up with a new reality, changes to society and in practice and research findings.

The Act's intentions are to:

- modernise and improve the legal framework for adoption and permanence planning;
- create greater long-term stability and permanence for children who cannot live with their families;
- improve procedures, services and support for adoptive and foster parents and everyone involved in adoption and permanence;
- ensure that Scotland's most vulnerable children have the protection and security they need; and
- create a modern, child-centred adoption and permanence service that responds to the changing needs of individual children. (Scottish Government, 2009a)

The most controversy generated during the Act's passage through into legislation was another indication of legislation catching up with developing practice — the Act allowed for joint adoption by unmarried couples (including same-sex couples) and fostering by same-sex couples.

Less controversial and in a more innovative capacity, Part 2 of the Act introduced Permanence Orders to replace freeing orders and parental responsibility orders. POs are intended to provide 'increased stability for children 'while being flexible enough to account for the differing needs of children' (Scottish Executive, 2006, p. 5). POs are designed for children who cannot safely return home, and for whom long-term legal provision is needed. They are meant to be 'final orders' in the sense that they provide legal security and stability for children who are to be looked after long-term and who cannot return home.

POs allow a court to allocate parental responsibilities and rights between a local authority, foster parents and birth parents as a court sees fit, allowing increased flexibility and recognising that 'for many children birth parents will continue to play a role in their life, even if they cannot live with them' (Scottish Executive, 2006, p. 6). POs may also be used as a route to adoption. POs can give authority for the child to be adopted or this can be added at a later date although POs are not necessary for adoption to go ahead.

The introduction of the PO is a potentially revolutionary move in that the choice either of long-term foster care with all its impermanence or of adoption with its finality may be a thing of the past. Time will tell. A third option, which is not so much an innovation as a renewed acknowledgement of the strengths and potential of family networks, is kinship care and this will be discussed in Chapter 4.

Finally, as can be seen from this overview of changes in fostering and adoption over the past three decades, there are many overlaps between the two fields, such as the emphasis on contact. In some cases there are gaps such as the relative lack of research, in the UK anyway, on how children assess their lives. An exception is the survey undertaken by the Commission for Social Care Inspection (2006), which is one of the most informative accounts of adopted children's views yet, involving as it does 201 children. It gives a rich insight into both life before and after adoption and is a recommended place to refresh practice if you are experienced and a good starting point if you wish to become a practitioner in one of the most exacting fields of social work.

CHILDREN ON HOW THEY FELT BEING ADOPTED

'Adoption is great and it's the start of a new life. It's fun and exciting';

'As long as the social worker picks the correct family for the child, the child will have a happy normal life';

'Adoption can be a scary, sad and happy experience'. (quoted in Commission for Social Care Inspection, 2006, p. 40)

Summary

As can be seen then, present-day developments in adoption and fostering are part of a long tradition of caring for other people's children and there are many interesting and potentially valuable initiatives underway. The next two chapters provide a contemporary picture of practice challenges and offer examples of best practice.

CHAPTER 2

Towards Contemporary Adoption and Fostering Practice

This chapter discusses changes in thinking, attitudes and practice that have led to where we are today. It looks at insights and innovations that remain valuable and gives examples of enduring good practice.

Changing attitudes, changing practices

As discussed in Chapter 1, formal adoption and foster care in Scotland has a long history in child welfare practice throughout most of the twentieth century. Significant changes in the traditional basis of secrecy in adoption, and the perception of which children might benefit from adoption and fostering placements, took place from the mid- to late 1970s. These were followed by a substantial amount of new practice, thinking and research interest during the 1980s, resulting in many older children and those with disabilities being placed in permanent family care, many with the legal security of adoption rather than drifting through their childhoods in large institutions or random foster care situations.

Rowe and Lambert (1973) identify what they termed 'drift in care' and their study was seminal in illuminating the lives of children in care in the UK at that time. It had such a profound effect because it was a stunning example of research that rang true for frontline social workers and managers. Rowe and Lambert's key points are:

- children who had been in care for more than six months had only a one-in-four chance of returning home;
- many children remained in residential care for most of their childhood;

- 22% of these children, in the opinion of their social workers, required a permanent substitute family. (Rowe and Lambert, 1973)

In the mid-1970s, the Scottish social work workforce comprised mainly 'baby boomers' who had been able to become qualified through trainee schemes and full-cost sponsorship by the government. These new social workers came from a wide range of social backgrounds and the lives of children in care presented a stark contrast in fate. A visit to a typical children's home presented the experience for the worker of often being surrounded by a number of children seeking attention indiscriminately. During this period, the possibility of deliberate abuse within care was not much acknowledged, while physical control and punishment were in any case expected and condoned. There was, however, a growing sense that the community could and should do better by children (Shaw, 2007). A further impetus for change for the new generation of social workers was the progressive principles of the Kilbrandon Report (1964) and the Social Work (Scotland) Act 1968, which, among other things, established the model of open-door services for families with the specific aim of preventing family breakup.

From the beginning of the 1970s, a mixture of preventative work with families and an emphasis away from 'the dorms and lights out' model of residential provision for children gradually resulted in children's homes becoming smaller ('group homes'). Foster care provision developed with an emphasis on local, community-based foster families, moving on from the earlier twentieth-century practice of placing children in rural areas, with the benign intention of them being in fresh air with good food, away from the pollution in the then heavily industrialised cities.

Improved training for residential staff also began to be expected in the 1970s and the Aberlour Trust, originally a large rural orphanage, led the way not just in re-establishing its care provision in a series of smaller urban group homes where children could be involved with the community, but also in banning corporal punishment.

This era also saw the development of preventive social work principles and practices, which led to interest in why children came into care. Previously, child care assumptions had been made that, for example, a father on his own would not be able to look after his children and that, unless there was a grandmother or possibly a single aunt who could do so, the man would carry on working but give up his children — there being little early years' child care provision. Child care provision for children was not then thought to be necessary because fewer women with children then worked outside the home.

Other triggers for what was termed 'reception into care' also disappeared. An example was a Housing Act in 1974 which meant that local authority housing departments became responsible for providing accommodation for evicted families. Previously, children would have been likely to come into care if their parents were evicted. And if a mother decided to leave her partner, he would have been likely to retain the council tenancy and the woman (often with children) would not have been able to access alternative accommodation. The situation also changed with the introduction of the Matrimonial Homes (Family Protection) (Scotland) Act 1981, which ensured an alternative to the possibility of children being taken into care in these circumstances.

The Social Work (Scotland) Act 1968 was implemented in 1971 and was another piece of legislation that could be used to prevent children coming into care, with its requirements to support vulnerable families. Section 12 of the Act, for example, enabled the provision of assistance, guidance and support to people in need, which included children up to eighteen, and became widely used as the basis for a range of preventive resources including financial grants.

At a broader level, local government reform in 1975 created regional authorities such as Strathclyde, Lothian and Tayside and set the scene for consistent, large-scale and imaginative developments.

Adoption: Shifting attitudes

During the period under discussion, the idea in the UK and USA of secrecy being paramount also began to be questioned and research on Scotland's adoptions, *In Search of Origins* (Triseliotis, 1973) was highly influential. Triseliotis' work challenged earlier notions about why adopted adults sought information about their origins — something had to be 'wrong' with them or their adoption. Triseliotis, himself an adoptive father, showed that, in fact, curiosity — the need to know where they came from — was the driving force. Acknowledgement of the need to know about heritage, along with harrowing accounts of people finding out about their adoptive status by surprise, had a profound effect on adoption practice and from the 1970s onwards adoptive parents were strongly advised to be open with their children about their adoptive status and, as knowledge grew, about the facts of their background, heritage and reasons for adoption.

Thinking also began to shift about there being some level of inclusion of the birth mother in aspects of the planning of the placement. Forward-looking practice in the 1970s might consist of a mother being asked for her views about the kind of family she would wish her baby to be placed in and being given some brief anonymised information about the adoptive family. She would be asked to write a letter about herself to leave for the child, along with some mementos, including photographs. A signifier of this change in thinking over the years has been the shift in attitude over time to naming the baby. Whereas it would have been usual up to the 1960s and beyond for the child to be completely renamed by adopters, it was now suggested that the birth forename be kept as a middle name as a symbol of the other heritage. Later, advice and even direction for infant placements have been to keep the child's original first name and include a name of the adopters' choice as a middle name. This is not only to respect the significance of the birth family but also to reflect current knowledge about the early importance for young children of their first name in their identity formation and imaging of themselves (Collins and Foley, 2008).

A major implication of these changes in knowledge about transparency and the additional psychological tasks in adoption was to initiate a review of what attributes were needed in adoptive parents, and how the rationale for changing thinking could be conveyed to them. However, it was to be a long time yet until the current common practice of encouraging initial meetings between birth parents and adopters, and even ongoing face-to-face contact, would come about.

A key development: The permanence planning movement

From the late 1970s, the new regional authorities' social work services began to address the issue of drift and quality of care more systematically and one of the strongest aspects was in setting up planning and placement systems to consider children perceived to be 'drifting' in care and what could be resolved for a better future for them. Much of the energy for the new approach was taken from examples of developing practice in agencies in the US, encouraging a rethink about who might have the motivation and potential to become committed to caring for older children.

This initiative was rooted in attachment theory ideas, which emphasised the crucial element in well-being of a safe, secure base of relationships, and the broader idea that permanence was about planning for where that child would be raised for the rest of their childhood, preferably being cared for safely within their own birth family. A clear principle of permanence planning was also a belief that older children could form new, close attachments which were nurturing and healing; in this, thinking moved on from the narrower original ideas that posited that children's attachment and relationship patterns were set from their earliest experiences of bonding.

Following models shared by US peers, most Scottish local authorities and some voluntary agencies such as Barnardo's set up teams to recruit and assess potential families, looking beyond the previous norm of childless couples with religious affiliations (also asking that older children be considered by such childless couples). At this point, the policy was supported by belief rather than evaluated outcomes. Subsequently, learning from these early more flexible approaches was widely written up in a series of publications of practice developments and research during the 1980s and early 1990s (Hill and Shaw, 1998).

'TIME OF CHANGE' — THE LOTHIAN REGION EXAMPLE

The key components of the Lothian Region approach, termed 'Time of Change' (from the late 1970s), focused on children up to twelve who were already in care, as well as those at risk of becoming accommodated. Key aspects were:

○ intensive work to prevent 'reception into care';
○ attaining return to birth family care without delay if a child was accommodated;

○ scrutiny of planning for children not returned to birth family;
○ planning for permanence in a new family if birth family care was not feasible.

Key outcomes were:

○ a number of children were able to be reunited with parents or other birth family members;
○ some were adopted by their then foster carers (using the new Adoption Allowance Scheme as financial support for this transition);
○ others found permanent carers, mostly adopters and mostly with reasonably successful consequences (Borland et al., 1991).

The disruption rate for older children in the Lothian study was found to be lower than others, and some of this was found to be linked to the open planning and decision-making system which included carers and children (for example, foster carers already caring for a child were included in the initiative as permanent carers or adopters, thus making a positive choice to keep — 'claim' — that child).

A particular insight that emerged, which led to further practice change and development throughout the 1980s and early 1990s, was an understanding of:

○ the benefits of maximising the potential of applicants through initial interactive preparation work: for example, in learning groups, reading and meeting with experienced adopters. The 'application to adopt' process was also enriched by the introduction of debates on what would rule applicants 'in' or 'out': for example, types of criminal record, complex health issues that would affect capacity to care; and
○ the need for flexible, ongoing and non-judgemental support being available to the 'new' families.

The Lothian family placement team proposed having groups based on adult-learning principles as a compulsory part of the preparation of adopters and foster carers, on the basis that it would be an effective, efficient and non-threatening means of learning and enabling reflection:

> I recall some social workers expressing the view that 'You'll never get working class Scotsmen to take part in groups.' This proved resoundingly not to be the case, with one of the professional rewards from this kind of work coming from seeing adults from the widest range of backgrounds finding emotional resources within themselves that they were then able to deploy to help children. (Hoggan — personal recollection)

During this period there were parallel initiatives in modernising the fostering service especially in recruiting carers to focus on the specific fostering task that was right for them. Some potential carers, for example, were motivated by interest in the challenge of helping adolescents to reach adulthood and a number of successful Scottish-based services were established for this group of young people. 'Teenage' care services led the way in paying carers a fee as well as an allowance for the young person, in recognition of the provision of care as an alternative to other employment that carers might have undertaken.

Thus, during the 1970s and 1980s, Scottish society, and social work in particular, experienced a general opening up and sense of energy in relation to adoption and the concept of permanent and task-centred foster care. In this process some unforeseen positive developments emerged. There were parallel social changes in the way disability was perceived, leading to the eventual closure of many of the large, rural institutions where many children had been placed for life (such as Lennox Castle, Gogarburn, Woodilee), and the move to community-based care or independent living. Some of these older facilities had children's wards, and as part of the closure plans regional family-finding services explored whether it might be possible for some of the children and young people to be placed in family-based care. The outcomes were more successful than predicted as it transpired that this call tapped into resourceful people in the community who had a positive view of disability; this was a different group to the poten-tial adopters or permanent carers whose motivation was to bring up a child from infancy or meet the challenge of helping a vulnerable adolescent. Some carers who came forward had been staff or volun-teers at the institutions and had an existing attachment to a particular child. Many of these children thrived physically as well as emotionally when they left institutional care and received one-to-one attention, affection and stimulation.

In 1991, Moira Borland and colleagues detailed the experience of eleven disabled children who had been permanently fostered or adopted; they were described as having severe learning difficulties, with six of them also having significant physical disabilities. (Children with moderate learning difficulties were included in the mainstream part of the study.) Five were over ten years old at the time of place-ment and six aged between two and ten; all but three children had spent all of their time in residential care, including long-stay hospital settings. The carer families were from a wide range of social and economic backgrounds and two-thirds had at least one carer who had previous experience of children with severe learning difficulties, including in employment, volunteering or offering short breaks (Borland *et al.*, 1991). This report, undertaken for Lothian Region, reinforced findings by Macaskill (1988) and Hill (1989).

These placements had such a high rate of stability that they were not included in the mainstream statistical analysis of the Lothian placements as they would have skewed the results. Virtually every child had become more confident and settled, and many behaviour problems had been overcome. Every parent mentioned the 'blossoming' of the child as a key reward for them, including them beginning 'to laugh and smile'. This is well worth remembering when we consider today that some children with disabilities or complex health needs are still placed in long term, fifty-two weeks a year, residential school care and thereby removed from family life. Unlike the restriction of liberty brought about by placement in secure care, which needs to be scrutinised by a Children's Hearing and possibly a sheriff, these arrangements are often made through an agreement with parents with the local authority funding the placement.

Legislative changes reflecting these shifts and initiatives in the 1970s and 1980s followed in the Adoption (Scotland) Act 1978, in 1984–5 regulations, then in the Children (Scotland) Act 1995, with its related regulations and guidance, *Scotland's Children* (Scottish Office, 1997). These introduced more direction, including:

- timescales for making individual child plans for looked after and accommodated children and reviewing these;
- the introduction of financial support in the form of adoption allowances; and
- the need for provision of other forms of ongoing support.

In decision-making through the Freeing for Adoption process there was a series of updated methods of legal testing as to whether adoption without parental consent was justified. The concept of the child's welfare and life-long well-being being paramount in these decisions was also introduced.

The measure of 'Freeing' was, however, experienced as unwieldy to operate by agencies and courts and was perceived to build in delays to

planning for children. This in itself led to some local authority practice in moving children to what were intended to be new permanent
families without parents having a clear legal way in which to challenge
the plan before it was implemented: for example, by effecting changes
of residence via the Children's Hearings system. Once the child was
settled, the 'new' family would then apply for an adoption order, or
the local authority would apply for a Freeing Order, with the court
being presented with evidence of a child now securely attached and
thriving in the new family. Clearly such practices marginalised birth
parents and this topic will be returned to.

Outcomes research on adoption and other permanent placements in the late twentieth century

In considering permanent family placement outcomes from this
period, most credible research relevant to the UK context found
that adoption or permanent fostering can provide a life-changing
positive opportunity for some children who could not be brought
up in their family of origin (Sellick and Thoburn, 1996; Parker,
1999). During the 1980s and 1990s, a substantial amount of relevant
research was conducted in Scotland (Borland *et al.*, 1991; Hoggan,
1991; Hill and Triseliotis, 1986; Sim and O'Hara, 1982; see also Robinson and Stalker's 1998 contribution to more detailed and positive
views of disability).

In quantitative measures of 'success' defined by the placement not
disrupting and lasting till adulthood, the rising age of the child from
infancy is one significant factor. Although the rate of non-lasting
placements increases to 20% or more from placement at mid-primary
age upwards, it is important to bear in mind that permanent placement, including adoption, can be very positive for older children,
including adolescents, when they feel that they have a strong voice
in the plan.

Three further factors consistently emerge as highly significant in
measures of 'success', which go beyond the single factor of the child
remaining in the family till the end of childhood in, for example, well-
being outcomes and mutual satisfaction, and this has been a particular interest of researchers such as Sellick and Thoburn (1996). The
first is the capacity of the permanent carers genuinely to accept and

be open about the child's dual identity and the importance of their heritage and past, thereby enabling them as parents to undertake the crucial role of supporting the child's knowledge and understanding, as they mature, of what has happened to them and the implications of their genetic heritage. There should be no forbidden subjects. This aspect will usually involve a commitment to ongoing connections with the child's family of origin, which may include future siblings. The second factor is the capacity of the child and primary members of the adoptive family to form a bond with each other. The rewards coming from this can sustain the family grouping in overcoming the challenges brought by other difficulties. The third factor is the more practical one. It is contra-indicated to place a child close in age or stage of development to a child already living in the family (around two years' minimum is often used as a practice guide). In addition, while adoptive parents carry full legal responsibility, the availability of flexible, ongoing support from agencies when it is needed, throughout the childhood of the adopted person, and beyond, has been found to be important in the overall successful outcome of these relationships. For permanent foster carers the proportionate level of legal security which supports shared decision-making in parenting and enables both the child and family to be certain of their secure status is important. Practices such as continuing a Children's Hearing requirement — which will mean the child's place of residence being reconsidered at least annually — are to be avoided.

In terms of characteristics of adopters and permanent carers, what we came to know to be key personal qualities are:

- an ability to provide safe care and individual attention;
- a capacity for emotional resilience — 'flexible but resolute' — is more important than family structure;
- a capacity to grasp the significance for the child of belonging to two family heritages;
- having a commitment to support the child in understanding their background;
- a capacity to work through any fantasies and expectations of the child;
- an ability to engage in preparation and ongoing work with their agency.

The other vital element was that the decision to offer care was at the right time in their lives.

These qualities are more significant than family structure itself (such as being a two-parent family, chronological age) and many single people or those in reconstituted families adopt or foster successfully. Childless, younger couples can also do well with older children. Being at the right stage in their own lives (for example, in terms of career aspirations, reasonable health and energy levels, acceptance of and recovery from previous distressing events and changes) before making this commitment appears to be crucial.

Options for different legal types of permanent family-based placement

From the beginning of the 2000s, much discussion took place on what should make the difference between planning adoption or permanent/long-term foster care as the legal route to permanence for a particular child. Schofield (2003) and Byrne (2000) make useful contributions to the knowledge base. Their indicators for adoption are that:

- the child does not have positive strong links or a constructive attachment to a birth parent or other primary carer;
- no birth parent is going to play a significant primary caring role in the child's life.

The same authors suggest the indicators for permanent fostering are:

- the child is over ten, has spent a significant period with the birth parent or other primary carer and has a strong and positive emotional tie to them;
- there will be frequent direct contact, including some caring responsibilities, and the parent(s) are committed to playing a significant shared parenting role in the child's life;
- the child is being placed with older siblings who may not wish or need adoption (the family and younger child may decide on adoption at a later stage themselves);
- it is extremely unlikely that the child will be adopted. Experience in the UK, for example, has shown that carers of children who have significant disabilities often prefer the level of long-term

support provided by the child retaining their 'looked after and accommodated' status. (Here, care needs to be taken that 'unlikely' is not code for the local authority's unwillingness to make sufficient effort to identify adopters: for example, same race adopters may need to be sought further afield.)

Post-adoption and foster care services

Research and practice experience in the late twentieth century illuminated the desirability of providing adoptive and foster families with a range of ongoing support services as and when was needed by them. Support services which have developed have been based on increasing knowledge of what enhances resilience. The works of Fahlberg (2004), Daniel *et al.* (2002), Rutter (2005) and Gilligan (2009) (see Further Reading at the end of this book) have been important contributions and influences in Scotland, and methods of delivering support have become more structured from the original basis of informal peer support groups and one-to-one social work visits.

Some of the common challenges arising are around the:

- child and adults not developing a sense of belonging or bonding with each other;
- adopters not being able to accept the child's dual sense of family and heritage;
- child not fulfilling the adopters' expectations;
- unforeseen events occurring in the family's life.

However, there have been some difficulties in establishing what is helpful and valid. There have been some problems, for example, in the promotion of so-called 'attachment therapies' and the vulnerability of adoptive parents, foster carers and their support professionals to pursuing questionable approaches in their anxiety to overcome ongoing behavioural difficulties in the placed child. This has been addressed by the governing and other reputable bodies of mental health professionals in the US and UK. Prior and Glaser (2006) made a significant contribution to clarifying what is sound knowledge on attachment theory and in encouraging resilience approaches which are well founded and integrate the role of substitute parents in the process of forming an adoptive family.

However, there remains a tendency to label children with quasi-medical terms and focus on apparent deficits said to be centred on the child's incapacity to attach to a new family. What is perhaps more useful is to look at the potential of the development of adult skills, in what is sometimes termed therapeutic parenting, and to apply ideas from resilience approaches of what can create transformational pathways for children who have had difficult earlier-life experiences (see Gilligan, 2009 in Further Reading). There can also be a tendency to generalise that all children in care have impaired development rather than to consider in detail the individual pre-birth and life experiences. A mother with drug use difficulties, for example, may have really tried during the pregnancy to remain 'clean', may have been closely monitored by health service professionals and accessed emotional support from other services, but may not at this point have been able fully to overcome her difficulties after the birth and to raise the child. Thus post-placement support skills have been refined over the past decade.

A sound practice example of post-placement support is delivered by the St Andrew's Children's Society in a structured programme 'Safe Base'. Key Safe Base parenting programme aims are:

- educate parents about attachment difficulties;
- help parents better understand themselves and their child;
- demonstrate practical Theraplay® techniques and empower parents to use these and other tools to change their child's negative behaviour;
- allow parents to meet others in a similar situation to exchange ideas and avoid feeling isolated;
- offer parents long-term support by providing online resources and access to ongoing links through family days, helplines and a worker when needed.

Whilst local authorities are required to offer support after adoption, some imaginative forms of help and support have also emerged from the non-statutory sector including adoptive-parent support groups, family therapy interventions and parent-mentoring schemes.

Adoption practice and ongoing contact

As has been discussed, the tradition of secrecy in adoption has all but been replaced (certainly for children in public care) with the promotion of openness by adopters to their child about the fact of their adoptive status and basic information about their background. Until about the mid-1980s, though, the general approach was still that one set of relationships with birth parents, and substantially with others, should end at the time of placement. This was in the belief that the child and the new adopters could then focus on their attachments to each other and that this would be hindered by continuing previous attachments (Goldstein *et al.*, 1973). This was the so-called 'clean break' approach about which some (but far from all) frontline practitioners felt uncomfortable because it meant forcing a child to lose all contact with relatives such as siblings and grandparents who were not able to undertake full-time care but who had done the children no harm and may have tried to offer what support they could. This discomfort was reinforced theoretically by some of the large-scale studies of adoption in the 1980s, which found that an open connection with birth relatives, whether by letters or face to face, could make a significant contribution to the child's ability to settle well. Another important benefit was that adopters were able to respond to the developing child's questions directly, and to find out more, since the lines of communication, records and therefore connection to birth relatives, had not been closed off. Wolfgram (2008) provides an excellent — and critical — overview of thinking and practice developments regarding openness.

Definitions of contact have also been evolving. The term 'contact', as it is defined in contemporary adoption, can cover a number of forms of direct and indirect communication between the child, the adopters and others. It may entail face-to-face meetings or phone calls at regular but not necessarily frequent intervals. Meetings can take place unsupervised or supervised, at child friendly venues such as leisure facilities or in a family support centre. Some adoption agencies run events such as a summer picnic which is used for contact. It can involve the indirect exchange of letters, audio/videotapes and photographs sent via an adoption support agency, in situations where it is assessed as necessary that the identity of the adoptive family and the location of their home are not revealed.

One of the benefits of some form of long-term contact is that it can assist birth parents and other significant adults in realising that the child is developing well and therefore either validate their decision to agree to adoption, or at least reassure them — if the adoption had happened because of family problems. For all parties, it can bring benefits in dispelling fantasies about each other and it reassures a child that a birth parent they remember as very fragile is well.

When ongoing contact became an accepted option in the last quarter of the twentieth century, it was initially easier to see the purpose of ongoing communication for older children who had conscious memories of significant adults. However, practitioners and researchers reported a pattern of unsettled behaviour and questioning about adoption often emerging at particular developmental stages even in children who had been placed as young infants and who were in all other respects secure and thriving. The work of Brodzinsky and Schechter (1993) suggest that it was understandable for adopted children at the developmental stages at which these problems were reported (i.e. around ages six to eight and then again in early adolescence) to query their background circumstances, as they attained more cognitive and emotional maturity, including understanding of difference. By this stage, for example, a child who had always been told he was adopted, and accepted this, would then realise that this entailed a difference from most of his peers and would be likely to turn to his adopters for an explanation; this would indicate a healthy emotional attachment as opposed to a problem, but it also means that the adoptive parents need to be equipped to respond openly, rather than conveying any message that their adoption is an unwelcome subject.

This rang true for many adopters and practitioners and, in turn, enhanced the development of an ongoing exchange of information between adopters and birth relatives, thereby enabling adopters to respond fully to a child's questions at different stages of their development: for example, 'What is my birth mum doing now?' A graphic description of this dynamic is given by Jackie Kay (2010), an adopted Scottish author. She recounts her panicky feelings at age seven when she realises that her mum is not her 'real' mother: 'It suddenly occurs to me that the Indians (on a TV show) are the same colour as me and my mum is not the same colour', but she is reassured by her adoptive mother's committed and informative response.

Where contact arrangements are set up, it is no surprise that participants report more positively when ongoing support is available at the local authorities and/or adoption agencies, which made the initial arrangements (Neil, 2002). A knowledgeable post-adoption support worker can assist the adults on issues such as appropriate and inappropriate content of letters and help the parties renegotiate the frequency and location of meetings if there is face-to-face contact. Counselling can be offered if any of the parties is going through a difficult phase. Even if there are good relationships and the family situations are stable, it has been found to be preferable to establish boundaries and protocols, e.g. not necessarily having each other's phone numbers, but communicating via the agency, so that relationships are not jeopardised by a sense of intrusion if anyone phones at an unplanned time.

Although there are debates in which strong views are expressed on openness, either that openness in adoption is wrong or that all adoptions should be completely open (Ryburn, 1999; Quinton *et al.*, 1999), recent research and practice literature reflect that maintaining connections of some form is now normal practice when children are placed for adoption or permanence and has positives for all parties if assessed and managed well. We have come to realise that the welfare of individual children and their circumstances needs to be paramount in establishing plans, and we are now more aware of the need for placing agencies to provide ongoing monitoring and be ready to provide support to alter initial contact plans after adoption orders are granted.

According to Smith and Logan (2004), positive outcomes in connection/contact arrangements between adopters and permanent carers and a range of significant adult relatives are associated with:

- mutual positive feelings which grow over time;
- 'permission' by a birth parent (and by implication other significant primary carers) for the new family to be the parent;
- open and effective communication;
- agreement over frequency;
- adults' mutual concern for the child's well-being.

Current research interest is focused on the long-term outcomes of contact/no contact, and on variables such as level, type and frequency of contact, and the implication of background factors such as abuse and neglect (see the material available on the website of the Adoption Research Initiative: www.adoptionresearchinitiative.org. uk/ accessed 5 August 2011).

The end of the century

Towards the end of the twentieth century, the permanence planning movement was running out of steam and felt stagnant. Demography had changed and there were fewer young children in care and therefore needing placed. Childless couples had more access to other means of forming families such as assisted conception.

On a wider level, in the post-industrial economic and political context, local government structures in Scotland were changed to a thirty-two authority basis in 1996. Many small authorities did not need a full-scale family placement service for their local children; there was no need-based or financial incentive to spend from the local public sector budget on recruiting fully from the area; and some of the collective learning and openness to continued improvement were lost. While some professional leaders took the opportunity of the breakup of large-scale regional control to modernise services, in other authorities there was an absence of adaptability to the new circumstances and a lack of a grasp of the implications of the new authorities being separate organisations. Scottish local authorities, for example, agreed not to charge each other for adoptive placements (unlike the other UK countries). This in the short term seemed a very good deal for the large urban areas in that they received free placements from their adjacent rural or suburban areas, but as need grew again in the early part of the twenty-first century this decision proved to be costly both in financial terms of purchasing expensive external agency placements and for children in not having access to care which met their needs. The political context of the move to privatisation of services also influenced structures, and a business model of foster care provision began to emerge — despite positive findings in the mid-1990s of high retention rates of foster carers in local authority teams and of the high quality of support provided to them by their family placement workers (Triseliotis *et al.,* 1999). At the same time, there was an overall decline in the voluntary sector provision for adoption in Scotland with no new providers taking the place of agencies that closed.

Summary

This chapter has discussed some of the key contexts and practice developments that precede today's new legislative and policy framework for adoption and fostering. The next chapter moves on to look at current practice and challenges.

CHAPTER 3

Current Legislation, Practice and Policy Issues

This chapter offers a practitioner eye view of the present legislative, policy and practice context and provides examples of contemporary adoption and fostering practice.

During the first few years of the twenty-first century, despite good practice in individual organisations, there was a sense of loss of focus in overall foster care and adoption approaches in Scotland. There were: high vacancy levels in social work, with the baby boom generation beginning to retire or in senior posts; and little sponsorship for training combined with the perceived low status and stress of local authority child care social work and the high employment opportunities in other careers. The emergence of new adoption and fostering legislation and policy guidance provides an opportunity to refresh practice and re-energise practitioners.

Whereas most Scottish parents and therefore their children were doing well, the problems of the significant use of drugs and alcohol by some emerged as a major social issue and the impact on children began to be acknowledged by professional groups and the community. This concern has fed into new guidance and policy directions, such as *Getting Our Priorities Right* (Scottish Executive, 2001), regarding children in substance-misusing households. Whereas the focus for public and political debate tended to be on whether and in what circumstances children should be removed from parental care, some senior social work and other managers, and inspection bodies, were concerned that drift once in care was returning with a child perceived to be safe when moved away from the family home.

Some in-house fostering and adoption teams had diminished and many fostering placements were being purchased from a number of new agencies being established in Scotland. While some of the new agencies offered placements for children with high levels of individual need, some of the provision tended to be fairly general in approach, rather than specific. It might not be clear as to whether the commissioned task was initial short-term care and assessment of the child or whether the carer was expected to contribute to work with parents on returning the child home; or if there was to be caring for children with complex health needs; or if there was the achievement of a clearly planned permanent placement. Some of the established voluntary sector agencies such as Aberlour, St Andrew's Children's Society and Action for Children continued to review and modernise the focused placement services they provided in response to changing need.

Similar issues about planning had emerged in the rest of the UK, and Tony Blair commissioned a Prime Minister's Cabinet Office Review of adoption in 2000, which confirmed drift in care had returned for those whose return to family care was not assessed as feasible (PIU, 2000). Fairly rapid shifts in English and Welsh legislation and guidance on assessment structures, decision-making and family-finding efforts followed. These included the introduction of independent, looked after children planning officers (known as Independent Reviewing Officers), court specialisation in family decisions, and resources (through the 'Quality Protects' and 'Every Child Matters' initiatives) dedicated to supporting innovative projects, and systematic large-scale research on what works well in support to parents (for example, effectiveness of parenting programmes).

Renewal and updating in Scotland at this point were slower and, although a review of adoption and other care issues started in 2001, the Phase II Report, *Adoption: Better Choices for Children* appeared only in 2005 (Scottish Executive, 2005), and subsequent primary legislation, the Adoption and Children (Scotland) Act 2007, was not implemented until 2009. A standardised framework for holistic assessment and intervention with vulnerable families was not introduced until the initial government-sponsored *Getting It Right For Every Child* (GIRFEC) materials were produced in 2005 (see page xvii). However, some local authorities renewed and reinvigorated their strategies both for vulnerable family support and their responsibilities as corporate parents, as in the Inverclyde Children's Champions Scheme:

> In order to take forward the Corporate Parenting agenda within Inverclyde the council has embarked on a children's champion scheme in 2007. This involves all members of the Corporate Management Team and statutory officers, seven in all, agreeing to act as children's champion for fourteen looked after and accommodated children in Inverclyde. The task of the champion is to act as a good parent to their allocated children and to have for them the same aspirations they would for their own children. (Inverclyde Child Protection Committee, 2008)

Although addressing drift in care in Scotland at a national level arguably lagged behind the rest of the UK during the first years of this century, other aspects, especially in changing attitudes to partnership approaches, were progressing and had a spin-off in debate and dialogue about differential quality of life for children in the community. A key example is the introduction of the joint protocol on domestic abuse between local authorities and the police, which has resulted in domestic abuse being addressed more systematically, particularly in raising awareness of the impact on children (Scottish Government, 2009b). This awareness is contributing to the developing knowledge about the previous life experiences of children who are accommodated and the effect on their feelings and behaviour patterns: for example, in recognising that the source of a child's wariness when adults have any form of disagreement may be that this, for them, has been in the past the precursor to violence. Substitute carers, therefore, can help by addressing this in a conscious and specific way in their own actions and discussions with the child.

Evaluating the quality of care

Interest in evaluating the quality of care provided in fostering and adoption, including children's own perceptions of this, began to develop with the human rights agenda, and arose, unfortunately,

from the findings of ill-treatment of children, mainly from historical cases (The Skinner Report, 1992; Shaw 2007). Legislation and
guidance have incorporated the principle of taking account of children's views in decisions (as in Section 6 of the Children (Scotland)
Act 1995) and is referred to frequently in the fostering and adoption
guidance (Scottish Government, 2011a).

Scrutiny of the quality of assessments of prospective carers has
been built up in primary legislation and regulation (see Scottish
Government, 2011a, Chapters 11 and 19). With the aim of objec-
tivity, each agency must have an assessment panel whose members
have a range of experience, including health and legal, who consider
the approval of carer assessments and, in adoption, the plan for the
child, and then make a recommendation to the agency's designated
decision-maker, usually a senior manager.

THE CONTEMPORARY FUNCTIONS OF THE ADOPTION OR FOSTERING PANEL

Based on joint knowledge, skills and commitment to understood values:
- to consider assessments and make recommendations to the agency
  decision-maker on the approval and registration of prospective foster
  carers and adopters;
- to consider assessments and make recommendations on permanence
  plans, including adoption, for children;
- in adoption, to consider proposed matches and make recommendations;
- to consider reviews of carers based on evidence of the quality of care
  and any significant life changes etc.

NB the panel's function is not to conduct assessment but to consider the
assessment work carried out by the applicant family and the agency staff.

An example of current criteria for eligibility for assessment of
potential adopters is that of the St Andrew's Children's Society:

- Couples and single people aged twenty-one and over. We do
  not have an upper age limit but it must be clearly demonstrated
  that the applicant has the space, energy and good health to
  meet the needs of children. It is likely that older applicants will
  be considered primarily for older children;
- Roman Catholic couples and single people for children of a
  Roman Catholic heritage;

- Couples and single people of all religious denominations for children of any religious heritage;
- Couples and single people of no religious persuasion for children where religion is not a matching consideration;
- Race: white couples and single people for children from a white racial and cultural background; black, Chinese and Asian couples and single people for children from black, Chinese and Asian racial and cultural backgrounds;
- Males and females who are married or living together in a committed and enduring relationship;
- Same-sex couples living together in a committed and enduring relationship;
- Single males;
- Single females.

Reasons for ineligibility or assessment not proceeding will include:

- an applicant has a criminal conviction of a violent or sexual nature, especially if that offence was committed against a child;
- an applicant, or someone else in the household, has a serious, life-threatening illness;
- an applicant does not have suitable accommodation that would allow them to care for a child appropriately;
- the lifestyle of an applicant was such that it would impede their ability to care for a child: for example, their employment or hobby meant that they spent a lot of time away from home and that meant that someone other than the applicant would have significant caring responsibilities for a child placed;
- an applicant has a child that they do not care for and is being accommodated and looked after by a local authority;
- an applicant has a child under five living in their household. (www.standrews-children.org.uk/adoption.htm; accessed 8 August 2011)

Formal arm's length bodies and systems developed in the 2000s with functions of inspecting standards of practice in child care services. Systems to evaluate standards include planned and unannounced visits by inspectors, scrutiny of records and service user feedback. Some expected minimum standards have been established for foster care, and adoption and any agency operating in Scotland (and UK wide) require to be registered (Scottish Government, 2008f). Until 2011, though, relevant scrutiny in Scotland was spread through three separate agencies, with the Her Majesty's Inspectorate of Education (HMIE) involved in child protection, including interest in the quality of longer-term planning for abused or neglected children; the Social Work Inspection Agency (SWIA) focusing on local authority child care planning and in-house services; and the Care Commission responsible for the registration of fostering and adoption agencies — public, voluntary and other agencies — as 'fit for purpose' but not for overall planning and outcomes for the populations of children involved. These agencies and their functions are now integrated in a new scrutiny body, Social Care and Social Work Improvement Scotland (SCSWIS), set up in April 2011, and it is hoped that clearer links can be made between individual quality of provision in care placements with planning for demographic need as it changes over time.

In response to the twin drivers of the *Getting It Right For Every Child* initiative (Scottish Government, 2008a) and the adoption and fostering guidance (Scottish Government, 2011a), practice is developing fast. In East Dunbartonshire Council, for example, when permanence away from birth family is being considered the child and family will already have had their needs assessed based on the GIRFEC well-being principles. Timescales for LAAC reviews would be based on the *Guidance* (Scottish Government, 2011a), but others will vary depending on circumstances such as how long it takes to identify a prospective family and legal processes (see Table 3.1).

Perceptions of children and young people
During the latter part of the first decade of the 2000s, the inspection bodies, particularly HMIE and SWIA, have been instrumental in encouraging expectations of focused planning by local authorities for individual children and consideration of outcomes based on well-being. The Scottish Government, via SWIA, published the views of young people who had recently been in care and who had a reasonably positive view (Happer *et al.*, 2006). Some commented that they should not have been left in their family circumstances for so long, and many spoke about the benefit to them of carers and teachers who stuck with them and believed in them.

Table 3.1: An exemplar of local authority adoption planning activities for an accommodated child

Stage	Activities
Professionals involved in the LAAC review of the child's plan assess that the child cannot return to parental, family or friends' care. Therefore, a plan for safe and legally secure alternative family-based care is progressed	Arrange a permanence planning meeting without delay to consider how to progress this plan. Remember that the timescales for becoming settled are crucial to the child and depend on professionals progressing their plan
Permanence planning meeting	Key professionals consider and record decisions and tasks including: ○ compilation of full report on the proposed plan and timescale for submission to the Adoption and Permanence Panel; ○ assessment of information by legal services in order to obtain advice on attaining legal security; ○ arranging a health needs' assessment; ○ progress of discussions on the plan with birth parents and other family members; ○ consideration of the connection with any full or half siblings; ○ discussion of the key characteristics of an alternative family for the child, noting any interest in caring from the child and how this will be processed (e.g. from current foster carers)
The Adoption and Permanence Panel and agency decision	The panel considers and advises on the proposed plan and makes recommendations to the designated agency decision-maker. Plan confirmed or not. Birth family contribute and are kept informed. Methods to identify prospective families progressed
The linking meeting	The key professionals consider families who are expressing interest
Placement planning meetings	Professionals discuss the proposed match with the prospective family, current carers and birth family prior to the panel
The matching adoption/Permanence Panel and agency decision	The panel considers and advises on the match and makes recommendations to the agency decision-maker who confirms or not[1]
The introductions planning meeting	Sets out the activities and schedule for the initial meetings involving the child, current carers, prospective carers, birth family, others close to the child
The introductions review meeting	Meets about midway through the projected introductions to consider progress, the views of all, including the child, and whether and at what point the child should move
Making the placement and ongoing support	Initial arrangements for visiting and setting up support networks

1   It is worth noting that the Guidance does not carry a requirement to seek the participation of birth parents in Adoption Panel discussions about their child although this is practice in some local authorities.

One of the few pieces of adoption research to engage directly with children who are still fairly young — rather than older adopted young people, adopters or professionals — has been by Thomas and Beckford in *Adopted Children Speaking* (Thomas *et al.*, 1999). This was of interest because, although there is much heated debate about ongoing contact, until then the views of children currently being affected were not heard. In this study, children commented that sometimes they felt that the contact that happened, but they did so on a grudging basis. They also highlighted the enormous changes it meant for them to settle down in a new home: for example, on moving, they had to 'meet new family, meet new friends, meet new cousins, meet new houses, meet new school. Everything really. Meet a new world'. The advice for professionals was: 'To know a lot about them (the child) could really help. Spend time with them.' Many of these feelings were mirrored in the views of an older group of adopted children in *Celebrating Success*:

> When asked what they wished that would change, the young people in the SWIA study responded:
>
> - don't let children lose positive relationships or contact with siblings;
> - don't leave children in unacceptable living situations for too long;
> - demonstrate personal interest — don't take them out to 'fast food' outlets if you want to convey this;
> - promote a more positive society view of young people who are accommodated. (Happer *et al.*, 2006)

Information from children in care has been an emergent and illuminating feature of the 2000s. A North Lanarkshire Council psychological service survey, for example, of forty young people aged between twelve and eighteen years old who were 'looked after and accommodated' provided these three simple tips for adults who work with them:

- helpful — was when adults listened and then arranged things like home visits;
- unhelpful — was when (professionals) did not turn up for scheduled meetings;

- suggestions — were listen more, tell the truth and give extra support at the beginning of arrangements. (North Lanarkshire Education Psychology Service, 2008)

Although the young people in the North Lanarkshire survey had criticisms of their care, they also seemed to be overall positive about their current situation. When asked: 'How cared for do you feel?' (on a scale of one to ten, ten being high), the average answer was nine. This level of positive response in one survey is perhaps in contrast to the received view of public care, but is largely mirrored in other local consultations such as East Lothian Council's 'Listen more, assume less' work (Department of Education and Children's Services, 2011).

Current policy and practice focus

In the second decade of the 2000s, the emergent policy focus is very much on the well-being of children and on maximising life chances. The current framework for assessment and analysis of the needs of vulnerable children and relevant services to birth families is set out in Scottish Government policy: for example, GIRFEC (Scottish Government, 2008a); *Health in Scotland* (Chief Medical Officer, 2007); and The Early Years (0–8) Framework (Scottish Government, 2008e). These and other associated documents (see, for example, those on the GIRFEC website) reflect the main knowledge and theoretical bases supporting the concept of establishing permanence and are rooted in attachment theory. Developing policy and practice are also influenced by the comparison of positive outcomes and resilience for children raised within acceptably safe nurturing parental or other primary relationships, with that of the poor outcomes and life chances for children who grow up without this base:

> At age three, children at higher risk of poor outcomes can be identified on the basis of their chaotic home circumstances, their emotional behaviour, their negativity and poor development. Without effective intervention … by the time such children reach adulthood, these children are more likely to have poor health outcomes, be unemployed, have criminal convictions, have substance misuse problems and have experienced teenage pregnancy. (Scottish Government, 2008e, p. 8)

The message is also underlined in the Chief Medical Officer's report:

> The lifelong ability (of children affected by serious parental difficulties which affect safe, secure attachment) to relate properly to others can ... be impaired and this will disrupt later ability to form relationships, to work, deal with adversity and also predispose to mental disorders. An insecurely attached child is more vulnerable than others to be the victim of traumatic experiences. (Chief Medical Officer, 2007, Chapter 3)

These principles and the practice changes and concerns that have evolved during the 2000s and been debated for so much of the first decade of the century are now codified in the Adoption and Children (Scotland) Act 2007 and the *Guidance on the Looked After Children (Scotland) Regulations 2009 and the Adoption and Children (Scotland) Act 2007* (Scottish Government, 2011a).

The Adoption and Children (Scotland) Act 2007

The *Guidance* document (Scottish Government, 2011a) relating to this Act is the one most relevant to practitioners and it is very detailed, covering: planning for children who are accommodated or looked after at home; foster care and kinship arrangements; adoption planning and placement; post-adoption support; and contact issues. Much of the content is the consolidation of previous arrangements — the welfare of the child being paramount, the function and role of adoption and fostering panels, taking account of children's views. The *Guidance* finally did away with the 1980s' ban on same-sex couples fostering and also now allows two people who are not married or in a civil partnership to adopt the same child together. The Act introduced another new form of permanence status which local authorities can seek in order to attain legal security for a child — the Permanence Order, which can be made alongside authority to place the child for adoption. The grounds for dispensing with parental consent via the PO and for adoption are based on evidence that the parent is unable satisfactorily to discharge or exercise those responsibilities or rights apart from contact and that the court must be of the opinion that the parent is likely to continue to be unable to discharge or exercise them satisfactorily.

Although the PO is intended to provide a fair but accessible means of deciding on parental rights, there remains a complex relationship between the local authority which is proposing the plan, the Children's Hearings system and the court. One of the original proposals in the earlier review, not included in the Act, was that when the local authority wished to progress a permanence plan for a child who was subject to Section 70 of the Children Act — a Children's Hearing supervision requirement with a condition of residence (which would be most children for whom permanence is planned) — the locus of decision-making should switch to the Sheriff Court. This would have meant that the sheriff would quickly hear evidence about the validity of the plan and birth parents would be clear about the implications. As noted, this is not the case and the process remains within the local authority.

The idea of the PO is to offer a flexible child-centred way of managing legal security; the local authority holding the order can delegate a number of parental responsibilities, ancillary measures, to the child's carers, or retain some for parents. Time will tell whether the PO lives up to its promise.

The Adoption and Children Act legislation and the regulations and guidance that flow from it are thoroughly and clearly explained in a helpful publication from the British Association for Adoption & Fostering — *Permanence and Adoption for Children: A Guide to the Adoption and Children (Scotland) Act* (Plumtree, 2011: see Further Reading).

Two future challenges for practitioners
Refocusing on identified and projected need
Recent signs are that local authorities are renewing strategic approaches to their policies on provision of placements and seeking to provide a coherent balance of quality in-house planning and provision, with more specific commissioning from the voluntary and not-for-profit sectors.

A good example is contained in the Edinburgh Council plan which analyses the projected need for adopters for young children from chronic drug- and alcohol-use parental and extended-family situations, and a forward plan to assess individual need and ensure sufficient suitable carers are available. This is reported to be progressing well with a revival in local recruitment of suitable adopters and other carers, including carers for seriously disabled children (Edinburgh Council Plan, 2009). In 2010, Fife and Edinburgh Councils produced detailed external-provider tenders for foster care and other services. These included specific requests for services for disabled children, assessment placements and clarity and detail about expected good standards.

Authorities are now reporting (in a personal communication to the author from the North Lanarkshire service manager in March 2011) the availability of reasonable numbers of foster carers and young child adopters, but they are also still needing to build up availability of permanent foster carers for the late primary age group.

The relationship between poverty and the need or desirability for adoption remains a complex one. It is unlikely that a parent based in Scotland would lose their child primarily because of low income or a very temporary troubled time; inspections and other research based on case file auditing and outcome measures consistently show that many vulnerable parents are offered a range of services which will often be of good quality and relevant. There are many examples of parents in dire situations being helped by professionals skilled in engagement and purposeful intervention, and thereby being enabled to bond with and nurture their child. The consistency and quality of effective engagement and skill will remain an ongoing challenge especially in a time of reduced resources, and professionals may not be able to help all parents with complex difficulties within the timescales needed for them to forge that motivating bond. This poses the issues of timescales (introduced to prevent 'drift' — which is where we came in), the nature and value of these, and alternatives to parental care where this is not likely to be forthcoming. The next chapter looks at the last with one emergent form awakening considerable interest — kinship care. Perhaps not emergent so much as rediscovered.

Continued 'labelling' of children in public care?
In theories of human development there has been a long-standing professional interest about the weighting of nature and nurture.

Related to this is the debate on the effect of placing 'labels' on members of the community who are different to the majority (for example, by ability/disability) and on the possible consequences for individuals of stereotyping and self-fulfilling prophecies.[1]

During the early twenty-first century, professional interest has been caught by emergent findings about the physiological effects of adverse early life experiences on brain development, with the beneficial aim of understanding how these processes work and therefore how we might best help children thrive. However, there is some danger that the topic is being absorbed by some professionals and family placement teams, and therefore carers and members of the public, as a fatalistic and pessimistic message. This may be generating a fear — as opposed to realistic preparation — for the prospects of children to recover from and thrive after difficult early life experiences. Despite the progress in knowledge about the therapeutic potential of caring members of the community, resilience and other strengths-based approaches, increased support methods and training for carers and adopters, there is the danger in the assumptions and language of children as 'damaged' and having 'syndromes' becoming a smokescreen used to avoid taking responsibility for believing in what can be achieved for children who cannot be raised within their families of origin.

LABELS — A CAUTIONARY TALE

Jackie Kay was born in 1961, the birth child of a Nigerian father and Scottish mother, and adoption was planned for her. Her prospective adoptive parents had had some difficulty in being approved in the late 1950s because they were Communists and did not have a religious affiliation, but were matched with Jackie in advance of her birth — unusual for that time. In *Red Dust Road* (Kay, 2010), her adoptive mother recounts that when the baby was born they were advised to 'pick another baby' as it had been a difficult forceps delivery which may have caused brain damage. However, the bond had been formed; the couple visited the baby in hospital and took her home five months later. If they had not done this, in 1961, it is quite possible that the baby, thought to have brain damage, would have been placed for her childhood in institutional care and termed as 'mentally handicapped'.

1 See http://en.wikipedia.org/wiki/Determinism (accesssed 8 August 2011) for more details.

Instead, Jackie Kay grew up in Bishopbriggs with her adoptive parents and brother, and has become Professor of Creative Writing at Newcastle University and a popular award-winning poet and novelist.

Summary

This chapter has looked in detail at today's adoption and fostering practices in the statutory and voluntary sector, primarily in Scotland. We have drawn attention not only to the emergent stress on evaluation by arm's length inspection agencies but also to the importance of children's assessments of their care. It is hoped that the new adoption and fostering legislation and guidance will be a springboard for a vibrant service that delivers the very best for our children and families.

CHAPTER 4

Kinship Care

by Maggie Mellon*

This chapter covers the development of policy and practice in relation to 'kinship care' in Scotland and discusses the benefits of the recognition of kinship care as a separate category of care for looked after children, and of consequent practice and policy issues:

> Kinship care is unique. It is not foster care. At the same time it is more than family support. Children looked after by kinship carers need the same safeguards as any other 'looked after' child but their carers will need a model of support which recognises the child, parents and kinship carers as part of a family system with its own strengths, networks and needs. There is a strong case for redefining kinship care as a separate category of looked after children. (Aldgate and McIntosh, 2006, p. 1)

The term 'kinship care' is now widely used to describe the care of children within their wider family or by close family friends. It is also used to describe the situation of children who are formally 'looked after' by the local authority and also that of children who are not.

It is estimated that around one child in seventy in Scotland, or approximately 14,000 children, is being looked after within their wider family, rather than by a birth parent (CAB, 2010). The number of children looked after by relatives is widely understood to have

---

* Maggie Mellon is an independent social work consultant, formerly Director of Services for Children 1st in Scotland. She was a member of the Scottish Government 'Getting it right for children in kinship and foster care' working group. She was also a member of the advisory group for the Kinship Care advice and support service run by Citizens Advice Scotland and is a former Kinship carer.

grown because of the growth of drug and alcohol addiction problems and consequent incapacity of parents. From a sample of 368
carers who phoned Citizens Advice for help, a third reported family
problems were the reasons for kinship care arrangements and that
these had come about because of the addiction problems of parents
for 36% of this group, and in the case of 25%, because of the death
of a parent. Three-quarters of the carers who called the advice line
were grandparents.

The number of children cared for by relatives who are not formally looked after by the local authority was estimated in 2009 to be
around 11,000 (Citizens Advice, 2010), while the number formally
looked after was around 3,200 in the year 2009/10 (Scottish Government, 2011a).

Thus many more children are being cared for within their wider
families than those who are formally looked after by the local authority. The support that children and carers receive varies across authorities and is usually, but not always, related to the legal status of the
children and whether the local authority has a statutory responsibility
for their maintenance and care. This is discussed in some detail below.

Support and care for children in kinship care who are not looked after

The question of responsibility for the financial and other support of
kinship care arrangements is one that is not always easily resolved.
Children who are not formally looked after, and their carers, are
not guaranteed any particular financial or other support or service.
These children and their carers have the same status as birth parents
and their children. The carers are, therefore, financially liable for
the child's care, and for any costs of seeking a residence order or of
pursuing the birth parent(s) for maintenance.

For those who are eligible for income support or other means-
tested benefits there is some financial help. For those on low incomes
or independent pensions, or with savings, there is an obvious and
quite serious financial cost in caring for relatives' children.

For these children, Scottish policy was made clear in the *Getting
It Right for Every Child in Kinship and Foster Care*, the most recent
strategy published on the issue:

The overall strategy for children living with kinship carers is set within the GIRFEC framework. The principles of 'Getting it right for every child' require that all agencies make their contribution, as required, to enabling the child to achieve positive outcomes. Children should get help when they need it. Help should be offered in a way that is child- and family-friendly. Services work together to ensure, wherever possible, children should be able to stay in their families where this supports their well-being and ensures their safety. Access to universal services will still be at the heart of a successful childhood. (Scottish Government, 2007)

From this it is clear government believes that most children in kinship care should not need to become formally looked after in order to 'get help when they need it' and that access to universal services is the main route for this help to be sourced.

Some local authorities have generous and wide forms of support available for families, which can help support children in need and their families, through the provision of free child care, travel, leisure, family support workers, community and other services. Others have less generous services, and ration preventive supports.

Many carers suffer financially from assuming the care of one or more child relatives, and feel that the local authority is taking advantage of their love for the children, where otherwise the local authority would have been liable to provide foster care or residential care and incur considerable expense in so doing (Black, 2009).

On the other hand, the very essence of kinship care is that of being 'family', of *not* being a care placement with strangers, whose only relationship to the child is through the offices of the local authority. The child 'belongs' and is not 'in placement' but 'with family' and in a relationship that will usually exist into adult life (Aldgate and McIntosh, 2006).

It should be noted here that, if the person looking after a child is not a close relative (brother, sister, uncle, aunt or grandparent), the arrangement for the child's care is subject to the regulations on private fostering. These require that the local authority assesses and monitors the care arrangement, giving written notice to the parent and carer that they are satisfied that the placement is appropriate and must visit no less than once every three months.

These regulations do not apply where the care is by a close relative, the degree of which is defined in regulation (Scottish Government, 2011a). This does not mean that these children's and their carers' needs for support and assistance are not the responsibility of the local authority, nor that any request for financial and other supports may be rejected purely because the child is not formally looked after. However, many of the kinship care groups that have been set up by carers in order to press their case for support argue that this is the case in many authorities (Black, 2009).

It has been argued that the growing numbers of children in kinship care whose main need is for financial rather than social work support points to the necessity for change in the national benefits system. The birth parents of most of these children are very often in receipt of or entitled to income support but cannot claim for children who are not living with them. Thus the burden falls on local rather than national finances, without any consequent resource transfer to allow for this. There is, therefore, a case for a non-means-tested national benefit for kin carers, which would financially recompense the carers on a fair, national level and would also relieve the local authorities of an income-maintenance role and would not require that children have to become looked after for purely financial reasons (Doolan *et al.*, 2004).

There should be no question of children becoming looked after by a local authority solely in order to ensure the financial viability of their care with a relative. Equally, the fact that a child is being cared for by a close relative does not relieve the local authority of the responsibility of making an assessment of their needs and ensuring that any necessary measures and resources are put in place.

Until and unless this case for a universal non-means-tested benefit is accepted by the UK Government, the Scottish Government policy is clear — it is incumbent on local authorities to 'get it right' for every child and that must include ensuring that care by relatives does not break down for lack of financial or other necessary support.

Trends in the use of kinship care for looked after children

The reasons why some children in kinship care become looked after and others do not are unclear. Most children in kinship care who are formally looked after are done so on the basis of Section 25 or Section 70 of the Children (Scotland) Act 1995.

Section 25 imposes a duty on local authorities to provide accommodation for children, if:

- no one has parental responsibility for them;
- they are lost or abandoned;
- the person who has been caring for them is prevented from providing suitable accommodation/care.

Section 70 is a supervision order by the Children's Hearing. Children subject to Section 70 orders are deemed to be looked after by the local authority, either 'at home' or 'away from home'. Therefore, only those children who are genuinely the subject of a mutual agreement of their parent and the kin carer would not be entitled to be formally accommodated and looked after.

The Children (Scotland) Act 1995, like its earlier counterpart the 1989 Children Act of England and Wales sought to introduce greater partnership with parents and families, and voluntary agreements rather than compulsory intervention to secure the best interests of children. Adoption legislation in Scotland has reinforced this, to the effect that an adoption agency must have regard to the views of the child, parents and any relatives and should not make arrangements for the adoption of any child where a practical alternative plan which would safeguard the child's welfare can be made. A court may not approve an adoption where this is the case (Adoption and Children (Scotland) Act 2007, Section14).

In government statistics, the categories 'residential care', 'foster care', 'at home' and 'other community placement' are used to describe the placement arrangements for looked after children. It is this last term — 'other community placement' — that mostly describes children in kinship care, but it also includes arrangements for some other children and young people who are looked after and are not covered by the first of the three categories: for example, young people placed in bed-and-breakfast or supported living arrangements, or occasionally in private residential schools. That kinship care is not a specific separate category points to the neglect of this area in research and in policy.

Until relatively recently there had not been much research, or practice and policy guidance, to support working with wider families in the best interests of the child. Supporting care by family, if the first option of choice, should be a strong area of social work practice and knowledge. Instead, it has been a relatively neglected area of policy and practice compared to the focus on stranger fostering, and adoption. However, despite official lack of interest in their numbers and their needs, the number of children in kinship care, including those who are formally looked after, has risen steadily since the mid-1990s.

In comparison to the number of children in residential care, which has steadily declined over the intervening thirty-five years, and the numbers looked after at home, which have remained steady, the numbers in kinship care and foster care have risen. The number in kinship care shows the greatest increase, and over the shortest period. The number of children placed with relatives (in 'other community placement') fell from 1,430 children in 1976/7 to a low of under 1,000 in the 1990s. In this century, this has meant almost a 300% rise from 1,200 children in 2000/01 to over 3,200 children in 2009/10 (Scottish Government, 2011b) (see Table 4.1).

Table 4.1: Proportions of children in care by type of care 1996–2010.

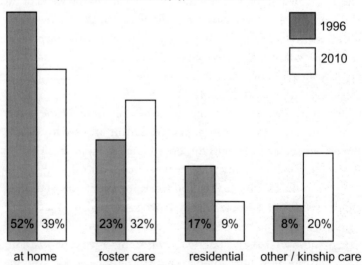

| | 1996 |
| | 2010 |

| 52% 39% | 23% 32% | 17% 9% | 8% 20% |
| at home | foster care | residential | other / kinship care |

It is not clear how much of the increase in the number of looked after children in kinship care may be due to a change in policy on support for kinship care. In 2006, the new Scottish Government implemented an election pledge that kinship carers should receive the same level of financial support as non-relative foster carers. This applies only to children who are formally looked after, and not to the much greater majority of children looked after by relatives.

At the same time, the Scottish Government funded the Citizens Advice Bureau to provide an advice service for kinship carer. Those assuming the care of children within their families would have been made much more aware than previously of the financial and other advantages of the child becoming looked after and may, therefore, have sought or agreed to formal looked after status.

In any case, the growing numbers of children in kinship care and the need for a more structured approach to their support have led to the development of guidance and policy on assessing and supporting such care for children who are looked after, and to greater clarity about the role of such carers, and their needs and entitlements.

Kinship care — a unique form of care
The report *Looking After the Family* (Aldgate and McIntosh, 2006) was commissioned by the SWIA in recognition of the growing numbers of children who were being looked after and accommodated within kinship care placements.

It recognised and focused attention on the value of kinship care for many children who are unable to be cared for by their birth parents, and called for the recognition 'in its own right' of this form of care for looked after children. Kinship carers, the report argues, unlike foster carers and birth parents, have not sought the responsibility of care for children. They have, nevertheless, assumed that responsibility, either at their own initiative or at the request of others.

Looking After the Family drew on research evidence from England and more widely, which found that children brought up in 'kin care' did as well as and better in many respects than children in foster care. The benefits identified in the report were that children:
- feel loved, valued and cared for;
- can maintain a sense of who they are;

- feel settled with people they know;
- have more stable placements than with non-relatives;
- are able to maintain contact with family and friends. (Aldgate and McIntosh, 2006)

Some disadvantages identified were:

- financial hardship;
- problems for carers having to cope with behaviour difficulties;
- overcrowding;
- ill-health of carers;
- inappropriate or less thorough assessments and minimal support from social work;
- children may be at risk from other family members;
- lower rates of reunification with birth parents compared to other forms of care. (Aldgate and McIntosh, 2006)

A recent study that compared kinship and stranger foster care of 270 children found that, while the children were remarkably similar in the two kinds of placement, kin carers in contrast were significantly more disadvantaged than stranger foster carers.

The children's outcomes in terms of placement quality and disruption in the two settings were also very similar. However, kin carers persisted with very challenging children in the face of birth parents' hostility and received fewer services than stranger foster carers, were more often under strain, and yet:

> children placed with family and friends do as well as those with unrelated foster carers but have the important advantage that their placements last longer. At present, kin carers' commitment and willingness to continue against the odds benefit the children they look after, but the good outcomes for these children are sometimes achieved at the expense of the kin carers themselves. (Farmer, 2010 p. 442)

These findings provide support for the recognition of kin care as a specific category of care, and for models of support for kin care placements which recognise their unique nature.

Kinship care recognition — 'in its own right'

If kinship care were recognised to be a form of care in its own right, the particular resources, benefits, knowledge and skills to support this unique form of care could be properly and appropriately developed. There are promising signs of the development of improved policy and practice in Scotland. This was recognised in a special edition of *Adoption & Fostering*:

> In the last few years, kinship care has risen up the policy agenda in all the countries of the UK. This is most obviously the case in Scotland, where the government has been developing a National Foster Care and Kinship Care Strategy. This process included the establishment of a task group specifically on kinship care that has produced detailed guidance on assessment and approval processes ... the task group also set out a 'vision' for kinship care and what needs to be done to realise that vision. (Hunt, 2009, p. 2)

Getting It Right for Every Child in Kinship and Foster Care (Scottish Government, 2007) confirmed the commitment of the Scottish Government to give attention to the needs of kinship carers, and developed further its status as a unique form of care, requiring separate models of support. This report is based on a set of guiding principles, the first two of which are:

- the needs of the child must be paramount and the child's preferences should be taken into account;
- unless there are clear reasons why placement within the family would not be in the child's best interests, care within the wider family and community circle will be the first option for the child. (Scottish Government, 2007)

Only if placement within the wider family is not possible should the child be placed with foster parents or with prospective adopters.

On the role of kinship care, the strategy states:

> The starting point in considering kinship care arrangements should be:
> - It is the right of every child to have their family and friends explored as potential carers if they need to leave the care of their parents;

- Any arrangement for care by family or friend must be in the best interests of the child;
- The safety and needs of the child in any assessment of family or friends as carers must be paramount;
- A child's needs for good family and friends carers should take precedence over the wishes of a parent to exclude the family from care;
- Support to a family or friend placement should be available when needed. (Scottish Government, 2007)

A family group conference (FGC) is a decision-making and planning process whereby the wider family group makes plans and decisions for children and young people who have been identified either by the family or by service providers as being in need of a plan that will safeguard and promote their welfare. More information on FGCs is available at the Family Rights Group (FRG) (www.frg.org. uk/ accessed 18 July 2011) and from Children 1st in Scotland (www. children1st.org.uk/ accessed 18 July 2011). The Scottish strategy recommends the use of FGCs in helping to make plans, agree support and assure the safety of kinship care. We believe that the case for a FGC could routinely be considered when:

- a child needs any form of help which depends on co-ordinated planning between professionals and the child's family;
- a child requires an integrated professional and family plan for rehabilitation to the care of his/her birth family;
- a kinship care arrangement is being considered;
- a child in kinship care needs a permanent plan.

The philosophy that underpins FGCs is inextricably linked to that of kinship care:

> The advantages of a FGC are that a child's wishes and feelings are a central consideration; that their needs for their wider family to be taken into account takes precedence over the wishes of any one member of the family, for example a parent, to exclude the rest of the family; and, if properly conducted and managed, FGC can reduce the number of meetings held for a sequence of overlapping purposes for the same children — a source of concern for many looked after

children. This is supported by both domestic and international research on the outcomes of family group conferencing in planning and supporting kinship care arrangements for children. (Scottish Government, 2007)

Directions to local authorities

Part V of the latest Looked After Children (Scotland) Regulations and accompanying *Guidance* (Scottish Government, 2011a) for the first time explicitly addresses the situation of looked after children in kinship care. For the purposes of this guidance, Regulation 10 provides a broad definition of a kinship carer as:

- a person related to the child by blood, marriage or civil partnership — with no restrictions on closeness of that related status;
- a person known to the child and with whom the child has a pre-existing relationship. This could include close friends or people who know the child well through regular contact and can be seen as part of the child's network.

Local authorities are required to:

ensure that their procedures explicitly address the needs of kinship care and have appropriate processes in place. This should include an identified point within the local authority for developing policy and monitoring progress. (Scottish Government, 2011a)

However, the Regulations can only apply to kinship care arrangements where the child is looked after by a local authority and, therefore, in a legal relationship with that local authority.

The definition of kinship carer when used in the Regulations is a relative or close friend who cares for a child or young person where:

- the local authority places the child or young person with the relative; or;
- an order by the court or Children's Hearing requires the child or young person to live with them.

This is perhaps not as helpful or as clear as it might appear to be. If a child is brought to the relatives' door at midnight by a social worker, is that a case of the local authority placing the child or young person with the relative? Many relatives have found that the local authority does not assume responsibility under these circumstances, with some reporting that they subsequently did not get any contact or support from social services (Black, 2009).

Local authority powers and responsibilities in making kinship care placements now include establishing a written agreement with the kinship carer. They also provide for formal notice of any looked after child in a kinship care arrangement to be made to the authority and health board where the child is or will be resident as a result of the arrangement. The placing authority remains responsible for support and supervision of the placement unless otherwise agreed with the authority where the child and family are resident.

Part VIII (Scottish Government, 2011a) sets out the powers of a local authority to make such allowances and payments as they see fit to foster carers and kinship carers — persons with parental rights conferred by a permanence order. This has the benefit of establishing that there is no definite financial advantage conferred by a child being looked after and that informal arrangements may be as well supported financially and in other ways in the child's best interests.

This is underlined by the *Guidance* (Scottish Government, 2011a), which points to the possible use of Section 22 of the Children (Scotland) Act 1995 to provide cash or kind benefits, and to Section 50 of the 1975 Children Act for those carers with some parental rights or responsibilities. The *Guidance* also usefully mentions the potential of one-off grants and payments for specific purposes and the provision of equipment, training, advice and other services to support placements. Such measures of support may be helpful to carers who would otherwise lose means-tested benefits if paid a regular allowance for a child.

Foundations of good practice?

It is not clear whether the growth in the numbers of looked after children in kinship care reflects an increase in the positive choice of kinship care for children as an alternative to foster care, or whether it reflects the overall growth in the numbers of children who are looked after.

The previous lack of support for kinship care of children might perhaps have been caused by a lack of respect for the strengths and resilience of families in adversity and to the family ties and bonds that compel many grandparents and other close relatives to take on the care of children of their wider families. The growth of kinship care in the context of the breakdown of care by birth parents is evidence that families in twenty-first-century Scotland have a much broader potential than has been recognised in policy that continues to regard 'the family' as consisting solely of parents and their children.

Getting It Right for Every Child in Kinship and Foster Care (Scottish Government, 2007), and the subsequent Regulations and *Guidance* (Scottish Government, 2011a), point to kinship care as the first and best placement option for most children who cannot be cared for by their birth parents. The foundations of good practice in supporting kinship care have been laid and may lead to a wider embracing of family potential and recognition of the need to support families in caring for their vulnerable members.

Summary

This chapter has discussed the reawakened interest in kinship care as a first option for children in trouble who cannot remain with their parents. It has outlined the obstacles and drawn attention to the benefits of looking to wider family networks.

CHAPTER 5

Adoption: A Life-Long Process

This chapter turns towards the implications of adoption for adults — and those children who have grown up in foster or residential care. Once they become adults, people who have been adopted, or fostered, may have a need to know about their birth families, the circumstances that led them to come into care, to be fostered or to be adopted (or all three). Access to information is discussed in this chapter as are the needs of other adults involved, such as birth families.

When a child and his/her birth family are separated, this has both immediate consequences and others that endure long after that child has become an adult. In adoption, as well as a vulnerable child who goes to adoptive parents, there is a birth mother who loses a child. Not only are there birth mothers, but birth fathers and other birth relatives such as aunts and uncles and grandparents who are separated from that child. In Scotland, between 1930 (when official records began) and 1991 (when a child adopted in that year would now be a twenty-year-old adult), there have been about 85,000 adoptions. This means that if each adopted person and two birth parents are counted, then there are more than a quarter of a million adult people in Scotland who are directly affected by adoption. If other birth relatives are added, this figure rises to such an extent that it has been calculated to be as many as one in ten of the Scottish population. If adoptive family members are included then, the figure is even higher.

What are the specific needs of these parties in adoption?

Adopted adults

> I don't know what diseases come down my line;
> when dentist and doctors ask
> the old blood questions about family runnings
> I tell them; I have no nose or mouth or eyes
> to match, no spitting image or dead cert,
> My face watches itself in the glass. (Kay, 2000)

Although the practice of openness in adoption has grown over the past thirty years, the fact is that many adults who approach after-adoption services today (because they were born in the 1960s and 1970s, and before) have grown up within a culture of secrecy surrounding their adoption (Rushbrooke, 2001).

Curiosity

Adopted adults' curiosity about their origins is an evidenced fact and has nothing to do with deficient upbringing and everything to do with a natural need to know where we come from:

> I was told at a very early age that I was adopted and that I knew I was very 'special'. However, it did make me different. As a kid I could never join in the conversations about who I looked like, whose eyes did I have, whose hair colour did I have, where did I get my features from? I knew I wanted to find out the answers to these questions, it was a question of when. (Clapton, 2003b)

Adopted people often lack genetic and medical history, as well as other family information. A routine visit to the doctor's office, where they are asked to supply medical history information, may make adopted persons acutely aware of how they differ from those who were not adopted. Furthermore, an inaccurate or patchy family medical history is not in the best interests of the adopted person (Palmer, 2009). More than just facts are needed. According to Neil (2000):

> It is important for adopted people to know not only the details of their biological heritage, but to explore the question of *why* they were adopted. This entails understanding

the issues that led to the adoption, including the circum-stances of the birth parents and the actions of social workers and agencies. (Neil, 2000, p. 303)

Neil goes on to state: 'the need to know the truth is compelling' (Neil, 2000, p. 304).

However, answers are often not readily or easily obtainable: for example, '70% of searchers and 74% of non-searchers said they did not feel comfortable asking their adoptive parents about their origins' (Howe and Feast, 2000). In Iredale and Staples' accounts of adopted peoples' meetings with their birth relatives, one adopted person feared asking her adoptive parents for information: 'I was scared of upsetting the apple cart by broaching the subject' (Iredale and Staples, 1997, p. 151), or, for another, raising the matter was at the least a 'guessing game' (ibid., p. 152). And in the words of playwright and adopted person Edward Albee: 'No matter how wonderful your parents are, what they give you and what opportunities they provide for you, they can never tell you who you really are' (Albee, 2006)

Even adopted people who are not curious about their origins have a need for services: 'Three-quarters (of the people in the study) felt it was right for agencies to let them know that a birth relative had made an approach' (Howe and Feast, 2000).

It is worth noting that adoption services are generally geared towards finding families for vulnerable children, and adults who have been adopted often find that obtaining information and ser-vices patchy and not straightforward — for example, they will have to approach children's services teams as if still 'children' — and it is not uncommon for adopted adults to be referred to as the adopted child when they seek to gain access to information about their roots (Clapton, 2008, p. 137).

Searching and contact

> Maybe I am looking for something I never had which I may never get, but until I meet her I will never know. I am hoping I can have a relationship with her. She is flesh and blood and there must be a tie … I've got lots of friends but I want some-body that is like me, that's *part* of me. (Clapton, 2003b)

Beyond curiosity, many adopted adults feel a need to meet their birth parents. The most common reasons given for searching for a birth relative include 'getting information about me to help complete the jigsaw' and 'the need to know more about myself and make the picture whole' (Howe *et al.*, 2001, p. 346).

The general rise of interest in genealogy and the ease with which searches can be undertaken have combined to fuel a rise in searches by adopted people (Clapton, 2010). Based on their research, Trinder *et al.* (2004) suggest that something like 50% of adopted people will seek information. And one researcher has gone as far to say that: 'We should perhaps explore why some adoptees do not search, rather than see it as a minority activity' (Selman, 1999).

Searching, and particularly first moves to broach contact, are very delicate processes in which the need for a place to 'stocktake' and have access to professional advice is recommended because the potential for disappointment at any stage is real. Armstrong and Ormerod (2005, pp. 21–2) provide a comprehensive list of emotions that may be experienced, ranging from shock to anger: for example, 'a mammoth shock' (ibid., p. 33). The search and contact process has been found to be more successful if an intermediary is engaged because this 'does give a better chance of ongoing contact being established' (ibid., p. 7).

Relationships: Building and maintenance

After contact, either by an adopted person or from a birth relative, people often need help with its impact. In the longer term, it has been noted that: 'People may need access to counselling over a period of years and not just at the point of contact' (Feast and Smith, 1995, p. 23).

Some studies support the finding of continuity of relationships after contact. Howe and Feast (2001) surveyed the experiences of forty-eight adopted people whose first meeting with their birth mothers was at least eight years previous and found that 65% were still in touch with each other. Triseliotis *et al.* (2005) found an even higher percentage of successful relationships when they asked ninety-three birth mothers (70%). In a large study of the key parties, Sullivan and Lathrop (2004) surveyed the views and experiences of 575 birth parents and 432 adopted people who had been in touch with each other for between twelve and twenty months. When asked about their expectations of ongoing contact, 94% of birth parents and 91% of adopted people said that they expected to sustain a relationship.

Kelly's (2006) study of relationships after contact concludes that for these to work they ought to be seen as a process rather than a one-off, big-bang resolution. This is a finding that is consistent across the existing research. In Browning and Duncan's (2005) survey of adopted adults who had been in contact for sixteen years or more with their birth relatives, they conclude that even after twenty-six years of contact many matters remain unresolved and that reunion is a life-long process. Another consistent finding is that there is no one post-reunion pathway (Howe and Feast, 2001) and no blueprint for these meetings or any relationships that may develop (Clapton, 2003a). Perhaps then we may conclude, in Browning and Duncan's words, that there is no convenient roadmap for the parties to these reunions, and we probably should not expect one (Browning and Duncan, 2005, p. 170).

THE EMOTIONAL EXPERIENCE

The complicated and variable feelings of all those involved in searching and contacts have been well researched during the later 20th century and findings are reflected in an article in *The Herald Magazine* (5/2/11) which recounts the experiences of three adopted people. There was variation in the degree of support and acceptance by adoptive parents in understanding their wish to search for information and try to meet up with birth relatives. What also varied was the degree of comfort or awkwardness in the interaction with birth family members with some forming meaningful relationships and others being satisfied with the new knowledge they had gained. One contributor recounted that it caused a rift with her adoptive family, while another, Chris Small, described how the support in searching he received from his adopters strengthened their bond further, 'The relationship I have with my [adoptive] parents has always been brilliant and they are my parents, no question... What's come out [of searching] is that I've become more content in who I am and I can talk about my adoption and the strength of my adoptive parents.'

Chris Small also highlighted the importance of the way in which professionals record family situations: 'The most striking thing (in the original records from 1961) was how judgmental the social workers were.'

Birth parents

Beginning with birth mothers, birth parents have 'come out' in the last thirty years. The publication of personal experiences (see, for example, Shawyer, 1979), the emergence of support groups such as the Natural Parents Network (established in 1987), and research in the USA (Deykin *et al.*, 1984; Brodzinsky and Schechter, 1993), Australia (Winkler and van Keppel, 1984) and three British studies (Bouchier *et al.*, 1991, in Scotland; Hughes and Logan, 1993; Clapton, 2003a, on birth fathers) have contributed to the present position in which the birth parent perspective and recognition of birth parents' needs are embodied in policy and legislation. The other dynamic that has contributed to the presence of birth parents 'at the table', including during adoption placement processes, is the fact that many children being adopted today are older and will have knowledge and experiences of their birth families.

It is the case that the majority of the literature has been concerned with experiences generated by the more 'closed' adoptions, which took place prior to the rise of more open adoptions in the 1980s. There is also a dearth of material concerning the experiences of birth parents who oppose the adoption of their children (Charlton *et al.*, 1998).

Birth mothers

Birth mothers need services that address the persistence of grief and continuing wish to know how their adopted children have fared. An Australian study of 213 women found that, while not all women experienced negative adjustment, for others the effects of relinquishment could be devastating and long-lasting. In particular, the study found that it was inappropriate to view relinquishing mothers as women who have put their problems behind them (Winkler and van Keppel, 1984). Subsequent studies in the UK such as *Half a Million Women: Mothers Who Lose Their Children by Adoption* (Howe *et al.*, 1992) underlined this message. At the time of its publication, a review of *Half a Million Women* notes:

> Previously it was assumed to be in the interest of all concerned for an adopted person's two families by birth and by adoption to have no contact during the transfer of the child from one to the other and thereafter to lead entirely

separate lives. For social workers there was no role after the adoption order since the newly created family merged with the general population, hopefully to live happily ever after. (Hill, 1992, p. 597)

For a birth mother, the adoption of her child can produce 'profound and protracted grief reactions, depression and an enduring preoccupation with and worry about the welfare of the child' (Brodzinsky and Schechter, 1990, p. 304). Other life events noted after relinquishment are poor relations with partners, or difficulty in making and sustaining personal relationships and alcoholism (Hughes and Logan, 1993). The publication of birth mother experiences has continued since these ground-breaking studies (see, for example, Robinson, 2010), leaving few in doubt as to the impact of adoption on birth mothers:

> Throughout all my meetings and discussions with the various people concerned with adoption, one message was hammered home more than anything else, 'Once he's gone, he's gone, you must forget him, out of your head, your life, start afresh, not for your sake but for the baby's sake, if you love him that is what you must do.' But there isn't a day goes by that I don't think and pray for my son. (Clapton, 2003b, p. 14)

Birth fathers

Insights regarding birth fathers have followed in the wake of recognition of birth mothers' experiences and needs. Since the late 1980s, studies of birth fathers in the UK, Australia and the USA have pointed to the many similarities of experience between birth mothers and birth fathers including: continuing to mourn the loss of their child throughout their lifetime; tracking the milestones of their child's life by imagining birthday parties, first days of school, graduation; and more. Attention has also been drawn to feelings of guilt and shame regarding the adoption:

> When you give up a child for adoption there is always sadness left and you have to carry this with you till you can have contact with them again. If you are a man then there is not much help out there. (Clapton, 2003b, p. 54)

Research on birth fathers has challenged the various generalisations and stereotypes of the child being the result of a 'one-night stand', or an older man getting a girl 'in trouble' and negative generalisms about men's attitudes to paternity. A majority of the men in Clapton's (2003a) study experienced feelings of fatherhood and a commitment to the mother. The birth of the child for most, even those who had agreed to the adoption, was an emotionally impactful event. During the adoption process, feelings of powerlessness and disenfranchisement arose and, for some, such feelings remained fresh and a source of some pain after many years. Enduring feelings of sadness and resignation were found in the accounts of a majority of the men — including those who had agreed with the adoption decision at the time. Feelings and thoughts regarding the experience continued as a source of discomfort for a significant minority throughout their subsequent lives. Such discomfort included a permanent sense of loss. And the adoption experience cast a long shadow over their personal, social and emotional lives afterwards.

Witney's (2005) explicit reference to *Half a Million Women* (Howe *et al.*, 1992) in the title of her paper 'Over half a million fathers' points up the many similarities between birth fathers and birth mothers. This growing understanding of birth fathers suggests that they need a service that understands that for many men whose children have been given up for adoption out of sight does not mean out of mind.

Other birth relatives need a service that appreciates their experiences, knows of the existing services and can advocate for them because, for example, siblings of adopted people have no statutory right of access to information that will identify their adopted sibling — even if they themselves were adopted.

Adoptive parents
Adoptive parents need a service that understands that the parenting they do is of value and that adoption brings with it specific and unique challenges, many of which are about how to acknowledge the importance of roots with their son or daughter and how to support them should they wish to trace their birth parents:

> Two significant themes emerged from working with children. Firstly, their sense of 'not knowing' about their birth

family, which occurred regardless of how well they had adjusted to being adopted. Secondly, sometimes very caring and supportive adoptive parents were unaware of their child's wish to talk or hear about their birth family. Parents misinterpreted silence on the subject of birth parents as a lack of interest from the child. Often it more accurately reflected the child's perception that their adoptive parents' silence was discomfort or lack of permission to speak or ask questions. Bridging this gap can only be to mutual benefit of adopted children and their parents. (Scottish Adoption, 2006)

Such challenges often continue or re-emerge when an adopted person becomes an adult and expresses a wish to meet their birth parents. And they continue through the search, contact and relationship-building process.

Social workers and other professionals

It has been suggested that, rather than an adoption triangle consisting of the adopted person, adoptive parents and birth parents, a better image would be that of a circle with a fourth party being the social worker. In services for adults in adoption, the role of the local authority social worker is less clear than at the point of the child's adoption, and often social workers can be poorly informed of the needs of adults in adoption and the services available to them. Accurate information on existing services, law and policy relating to adults in adoption is a must. Also essential is the ability (and skill) to give advice on the practicals such as how to access public records, searching and contact. Social workers need a service that can pinpoint the whereabouts of the adoption records of someone with whom they are working. They and counsellors and those working in mental health fields will benefit from regular updates in a fast-moving field: for example, the connections between adoption and later-life relationships, well-being and esteem.

Post-adoption and after-adoption services

Post-adoption support is normally understood to mean services that relate to the period after adoption to support the adoptive family and child. Arrangements for post-adoption support are now required to be in place, and local authorities may provide these or they may be delivered on their behalf by agencies such as Scottish Adoption Advice Service. Services can include family work, support with schooling and behavioural problems, one-to-one child counselling and therapy, and help with contact arrangements. Partly because of lobbying by adoptive parents. there has been a growing awareness that there needs to be a more open-door, return-anytime approach to post-adoption services and that an adoptive family may need help for years in meeting the challenges of attachment, maturation and identity formation that often come with being a child adopted from care. However, services can be patchy and over-subscribed.

After-adoption services are characterised by being distinctly for adults in adoption (adopted people as well as birth relatives and adoptive parents of an adopted adult). These services include: how to access information such as birth certificates and adoption records; counselling and advice; search, tracing and intermediary (go-between) services; and help with meetings, contact and post-contact between adopted adults and birth relatives. The work is generally undertaken by non-statutory agencies such as Birthlink and in the west of Scotland by Scottish Adoption Advice Service, which also runs support groups for adopted people. Other agencies such as Scottish Adoption in Edinburgh, St Andrew's Children's Society also in Edinburgh and St Margaret's Children and Family Care Society in Glasgow provide services for those who have been adopted by that agency. Scottish Adoption also holds the adoption records of other agencies such as the Church of Scotland and Lothian Region Social Work Department. It remains to be seen whether the Adoption and Children (Scotland) Act 2007 will impact on the quality of services provided by statutory agencies. However, at present it is fair to say that, as for services to adoptive families and children, these range in availability, standard and length of time before a request may be allocated.

Adults who have been in care

Who placed me in care and why?

Why did no one visit me?

Who were my real parents?

Who arranged for my foster parents to care of me?

Which social work department was involved, and how were decisions made to keep me in care? (Parliament of Australia, 2004, Chapter 9)

There are at least 300,000 adults who have been in some form of public care in the UK. This can range from days and weeks to years in various forms of care such foster care and residential homes, often alternating between the different options.

Adults who have been in care share many common needs with adopted people such as issues of identity and information relating to their families of origin, yet there is very little assistance available for these people if help is needed to find information about their past or tracing estranged family members (Feast, 2010). This group of people may have had to come to terms with considerable change and transition in their lives, and help is often essential if they need to move on in their adult lives (Goddard *et al.,* 2008). Loss in all its forms may feature highly, as does a sense of feelings being overlooked:

> Theresa's younger brothers were placed elsewhere, and she had little contact with them as they grew up. This was all the more painful as she had been responsible for much of their care while their parents were drinking, and therefore she lost an important role and sense of being needed. Theresa felt that the loss she experienced was not recognised by her social worker or the staff in her residential unit, and that she was not given appropriate help to come to terms with this: 'I grieved for my wee brothers. I still grieve for my wee brothers. I mean my wee brother is 22 but I still haven't got over the loss.' (Happer *et al.,* 2006, p. 24)

Information from records can explain why an individual came into care and the decisions that were made about them. This can help the post-care adult have a greater understanding of their family background, and enable them to make sense of their identity and history. Yet information is hard to access and at best can be patchy. Norfolk Council, for example, admitted to having been unable to meet more than one-third of its requests for access to files by former care adults between 2000 and 2006 because their files had been destroyed (Revans, 2007).

Even more serious, until the early 1980s it was standard practice, according to Quarriers chief executive Phil Robinson, for any child taken into care in Scotland not to be told that they had siblings. The theory was that the family the child had been removed from was deemed so damaging to them that it was better that all ties were severed. At the very worst estimates, Quarriers says this could mean there are up to 100,000 children who went through the system from the 1900s to the early 1980s and were never told that they had siblings. Although many of these people may well have died, tens of thousands of men and women aged from their mid-thirties and up are still alive and have no knowledge of their 'lost' families (Mackay, 2003).

The picture for Scottish services for adults who have been in care is unclear and is made complex by the sheer number of agencies, people and homes involved. It is also the case that an individual child may have experienced multiple moves during their time in care. These might also include moves between foster carers and children's homes. The only consistency is that records vary. Some more recent records run to hundreds of pages, whilst others from the 1940s consist of one page. Agencies and residential establishments have closed and, in some, records have been destroyed. On a positive note, the authors are aware of a number of care record-holders that take seriously their responsibilities to those who have been in their care. Quarriers has a dedicated service available, and we are aware of a local authority that prioritises this work, even, where possible, ensuring that the original social worker has input. Birthlink operates Care Connect, which offers a Scottish-wide advice and support service to those who have been in care, and has contracted with a local council to meet demands of its former care residents.

What is emerging is that the central needs, initially anyway, of those who have spent time in care are to make sense of their past, checking memories and experiences, filling in blanks. This can be painful, but as for adopted people necessary in completing a personal jigsaw. It follows that help during this process requires considerable skills, particularly in interpreting records. Finally, in this discussion of the needs of adults who have been fostered or grown up in residential care, it is worthwhile noting that care records are only part of the jigsaw. Former foster carers and care-home staff (even if retired or very elderly) may be the sources of vital information to fill in any of the blanks that may exist in the care history of an adult.

Summary

This chapter has identified the various parties affected by adoption and fostering, particularly focusing on the needs of adults. It has also discussed the challenges for practitioners and outlined the main services available.

CHAPTER 6

Afterword: Looking to the Future for Adoption & Fostering in Scotland

This chapter identifies some of the key gaps in our knowledge and practice base and looks forward to the development of a healthy and dynamic Scottish adoption and fostering service.

In their brief review of thirty years of Scottish adoption and fostering, Maclean and Hudson note that: 'A characteristic of developments in foster care and adoption since 1999 is that they have been mainly government or government agency rather than practitioner or academic led (Maclean and Hudson, 2010, p. 22)

We hope that this book will be part of such a development, and we finish on suggestions for improving Scottish adoption and fostering services, some of which will involve monitoring and evaluating new initiatives such as the Permanence Orders and the reawakened interest in kinship care. There are other areas of concern that we have known about for some time — for example, consistent support for adoptive parents — and these offer much scope to develop a uniquely Scottish body of knowledge and good practice. Here are our choices for enriching practice and benefiting the lives of children and families in Scotland.

Outcomes

In Chapter 1 we quoted Little's cautionary remark: 'There are few greater intrusions into a child's life than separation from parents'. In the same piece he goes on to note that 'there is not a single indication that placing a child in care improves or makes worse that child's health, education, behaviour or any other aspect of their development (Little, 2005, p. 17).

Surprisingly after more than a century of formal public care, debates still rage over whether behaviour problems are a result of the experience of care, or pre-existed and not been subject to change by care, and that later-life difficulties would have occurred irrespective of being in care. Equally, although we have much testimony (bad and good) as to experiences of being in care, we don't know whether a 'successful' life as an adult is as a result of separation from family of origin. In research terms, no study has followed a cohort of children from the point they entered care into later-life (Little, 2005). Also thin on the ground is our knowledge of outcomes for young children who have been adopted from care (Rushton, 2004) and the educational outcomes of adopted children (Phillips, 2007).

We are also underinformed regarding knowledge of outcomes and best practice in the case of children who return to their families after a period in care:

> We know what can go wrong when looked after children return home, we know much less about what works for them. The outcomes for children who return home could be enhanced by research which could tell us what helps to children and their families when authorities are planning their return home. (SWIA, 2006, p. 105)

Adoption disruption

Randall (2009) notes that there is no regular and consistent national measure of disruptions of adoptions from care. There appears to be no centrally kept figure of such disruptions — perhaps because agreement on what is meant by disruption has yet to take place. Coakley and Berrick have begun work on a common definition that 'would allow scholars and practitioners to interpret research more easily and to develop trend lines that are meaningful' (Coakley and Berrick, 2008, p. 1). They recommend three terms: 1. 'Pre-finalised adoption disruption' for placement breakdowns before the legal finalisation; (2) 'Adoption disruption' for use after legal finalisation; and (3) (the least precise term): 'That cases in which the legal relationship between the adoptive family and the adoptee is modified, terminated or set aside be termed adoption dissolution.' In the last case, a 'terminated' or 'set aside' adoption strikes us as final enough to come into category (2).

The question of the care-careers of children who are adopted from care, whose adoptions breakdown irrevocably, is underresearched (do agencies have practices and policies regarding informing the birth families when these events occur?). Coakley and Berrick conclude:

> From the child's perspective, however, any or all of these disrupted relationships could prove hazardous to his/her short- and long-term well-being. Stronger efforts by the research community to examine the long-range outcomes of children's connections to, and disconnections from, alternative families could be instructive. (Coakley and Berrick, 2008, p. 110)

The Scottish Social Work Inspection Agency notes that there is broad agreement that at least a third of all adoptions of children over the age of nine break down within two years (SWIA, 2006, p. 43). A variation in adoption breakdown rates depending upon the agency has been claimed by Scottish Voluntary Adoption Agencies, which remark 'that the disruption rate to placements in the voluntary sector sits between 4–8% as compared to a national figure of around 20%' (Scottish Voluntary Adoption Agencies, 2009, p. 3). This is interesting and might be to do with the additional post-adoption support that is perceived to be available at non-statutory agencies. This seems to us to be an obvious field of enquiry.

Contact

At first glance, the sheer volume of research, information, guidance etc. on parental and birth family contact with children in foster care or who have been adopted seems overwhelming. And yet, according to Triseliotis: 'The details surrounding (the introduction of direct contact), which affects thousands of children each year, remain underresearched' (Triseliotis, 2010, p. 59). This contribution in the recent commemorative edition (1980–2010) of *Adoption & Fostering* makes refreshing reading and, without reproducing the entire piece, it is worthwhile highlighting his thesis that, although the practice of contact has been promoted and developing over the past twenty years, when it comes to resources such as arrangements, preparation and debriefing of all the parties involved (for example, the child, foster parents, adoptive parents), the birth parents and other birth family members appear to receive the least attention:

> The 'promotion' of contact would also imply preparing parents and explaining why their visits are important to their children, how they might use contact more productively and how they would be judged. But no preparatory arrangements appear to exist. (Triseliotis, 2010, p. 60)

Triseliotis argues that such inequity can have far-reaching consequences, because how a parent behaves during a contact session might contribute to a judgement that means permanent separation from their child, and he concludes:

> Possibly the most contentious issue regarding contact and its frequency has to do with when it is justified to reduce or even stop it altogether and who makes that decision. Considering the thousands of children affected, research-based guidance is sparse. (ibid, p. 62)

Triseliotis notes that we have still much to learn about whom contact is for and its purpose and other more concrete questions such as how to organise it and where contact should take place. He also notes that broader questions of how to interpret what occurs during contact meetings, and whether it benefits a particular child, remain underresearched.

Children's involvement

Again, in an area where there would appear to be some satisfaction, it seems that contemporary practice falls short of the best possible. In the same edition of *Adoption & Fostering* as Triseliotis on contact, McLeod (2010) reviews our knowledge and practice base in relation to the involvement of looked after children in planning and decision-making and draws attention to shortcomings. She cites recent studies that draw attention to lack of meaningful participation in care planning, reviews and care proceedings. She goes on to speculate as to why this remain the case and why many children still feel that their social workers do not listen to them or give them the information and explanations they need: 'Why should practice still lag behind theory and aspiration? It may not just be that practitioners lack skills in communicating with children.' McLeod cites one piece of recent research (Archard and Skivenes, 2009) that found, although social workers made efforts to elicit children's views, they then often discounted them, arguing that the child was not competent to make the relevant decision (2010, p. 69).

A Who Cares? Scotland (2010) survey reaffirms this sobering glimpse of the state of practice in the inclusion of children when it drew attention to an absence of involvement in decisions to move placement.

Filial deprivation

The parents of children who come into care are a key set of service users. They are the subject of considerable attention (support and assessment) prior to their child's admission and during the decision-making process relating to permanent plans for the child. However, we know much less about their feelings, views and experiences after they and their child have been separated.

Almost forty years ago researchers in the USA coined the term 'filial deprivation' in relation to parents who had been separated from their children. Jenkins and Norman undertook a study of over 400 parents whose children had been taken into care. The rationale was that whilst:

> the effect of maternal deprivation on children has been a subject for major research investigation, the reciprocal aspect of the placement transaction, referred to here as filial deprivation, has not been similarly studied. (Jenkins and Norman, 1972, p. 97)

They found that the immediate feelings of the parents on separation 'ran the gamut from sadness to relief, from shame to anger, from bitterness to thankfulness'. The thankfulness related to an element of proactive volition on the part of the parents.

Overall, Jenkins and Norman found evidence of generalised attitudes of unworthiness or alienation and a sense of failure, noting that 'parenthood is a responsibility of our culture, and placement (i.e. separation) tends to be an admission that individuals have failed as parents' (ibid., p. 104). They suggest that there is a double sense of failure — a failure in responsibility, first as a parent and then as an individual (ibid., pp. 103–4). Other feelings are in evidence and these include 'interpersonal hostility, separation anxiety with sadness and self-denigration' (ibid., p. 267). More recently, again in the USA, researchers have confirmed much of the findings of Jenkins and Norman:

> We see from this and prior research that parents who must rely on others to raise their children experience feelings of loss and challenges in establishing or re-establishing a positive role in their children's lives. Understanding that at least some parents who are unable to raise their children for a period of time have strengths to draw upon could be useful to child protection caseworkers working with children in foster care and formal kinship care placements. (Gleeson and Seryak, 2010, p. 95)

Although some work in this field has taken place elsewhere in the UK (Thorpe, 1980), our knowledge is sparse. This is surely an area for greater enquiry given that these parents will be the subject of contact arrangements and efforts to reunify them with their children, have some continued contact throughout the child's life in care (including as part of an adoptive family) or be the people to whom the young person returns after care. Little (2005, p. 18) remarks: 'What little we know about separation is focused on the child. But what are the effects on the adult, and how do these effects then influence children's outcomes?'

Minority ethnic groups

The profile of children in foster care in Scotland is culturally more diverse than the foster carers, with 2.5% of children from an ethnic background other than British while only 0.6% of foster carers are from other cultures or communities (The Fostering Network, 2005, p. 5). Very little adoption and fostering-focused research has taken place among Scotland's minority ethnic groups with the work of Singh (1997, 2005) being a notable exception.

Summary

This chapter's brief (and selective) round-up of some of the areas in which our knowledge and practice seem to be lacking points towards some challenging and interesting fields of enquiry and research in Scottish adoption and fostering policy and practice.

If, as Maclean and Hudson remark, the recent period in Scotland has been marked by top-down initiatives, then the time seems to be ripe for the restoration of what they describe as 'energetic and pioneering practice, strong partnerships between practitioners and researchers and support for innovation from government and employers' (2010, p. 23).

We couldn't agree more and we look forward to a caring, professional and dynamic Scottish adoption and fostering service.

REFERENCES

Abrams, L. (1998) *The Orphan Country: Children of Scotland's Broken Homes, 1845 to the Present*, Edinburgh: John Donald

Action for Children (2009) *As Long As It Takes: A New Politics for Children*, Watford: Action for Children

Adie, K. (2005) *Nobody's Child*, London: Hodder & Stoughton

Albee, E. (2006) speech at 'Shedding light on the adoption experience V' conference, New York

Aldgate, J. and McIntosh, M. (2006) *Looking After the Family: A Study of Children Looked after in Kinship Care in Scotland*, Edinburgh: SWIA

Archard, D. and Skivenes, M. (2009) 'Hearing the child', *Child & Family Social Work*, Vol. 14, No. 4, pp. 391–9

Armstrong, S. and Ormerod, T. (2005) *Intermediary Services in Post Adoption Reunion*, New South Wales, Australia: The Benevolent Society

Ball, C. (2002) 'Regulating inclusivity: Reforming adoption law for the 21st century', *Child & Family Social Work*, Vol. 7, pp. 285–96

Berridge, D. (2005) 'Fostering now: Messages from research: A summary', *Adoption & Fostering*, Vol. 29, No. 4, pp. 6–8

Biehal, N. (2007) 'Reuniting children with their families: Reconsidering the evidence on timing, contact and outcomes', *British Journal of Social Work*, Vol. 37, No. 5, pp. 807–23

Black, A. (2009) 'Kinship care: Current Scottish dilemmas and some proposals for the future', *Adoption & Fostering*, Vol. 33, No. 3, pp. 40–50

Borland, M., O'Hara, G. and Triseliotis, J. (1991) 'Placement outcomes for children with special needs', *Adoption & Fostering*, Vol. 15, No. 2, pp. 18–28

Bouchier, P., Lambert, L. and Triseliotis, J. (1991) *Parting with a Child for Adoption: The Mother's Perspective*, London: BAAF

Brammer, A. (2009) *Social Work Law*, Harlow, Essex: Pearson

Brodzinsky, A. (1993) 'Surrendering an infant for adoption: The birth mother experience', in Brodzinsky, D. and Schechter, M. (eds) (1993), *The Psychology of Adoption*. New York: Oxford University Press

Brodzinsky, D. and Schechter, M. (eds) (1993) *The Psychology of Adoption*, New York: Oxford University Press

Browning, J. and Duncan, G. (2005) 'Family membership in post-reunion adoption narratives', *Social Policy Journal of New Zealand*, Vol. 26 (November), pp. 151–72

Bullock, R., Courtney, M., Parker, R., Sinclair, I. and Thoburn, J. (2006) 'Can the corporate state parent?', *Adoption & Fostering*, Vol. 30, No. 4, pp. 6–19

Byrne S. (2000) *Linking and Introductions: Helping Children Join Adoptive Families*, London: BAAF

CAB (2010) *Relative Value: The Experiences of Kinship Carers Using the Scottish CAB Service*, Edinburgh: Scottish Citizen's Advice Bureau

Charlton, L., Crank, M., Kansara, K. and Oliver, C. (1998) *Still Screaming: Birth Parents Compulsorily Separated from Their Children*, Manchester: After Adoption

Chief Medical Officer (2007) *Health in Scotland 2006: Annual Report of the Chief Medical Officer*, Edinburgh: Scottish Government

City of Edinburgh (2009) *Council Plan*, Edinburgh: City of Edinburgh Council

City of Edinburgh Council (2006) *Submission to Education Committee*, during passage of Adoption and Children (Scotland) Bill. Available at URL: www. scottish.parliament.uk/business/committees/education/inquiries/adopt/ ed06-adoptionbill-evid.htm (accessed 18 July 2011)

Clapton, G. (2003a) *Birth Fathers and Their Adoption Experiences*, London: Jessica Kingsley

Clapton, G. (2003b) *Relatively Unknown: A Year in the Life of the Adoption Contact Register for Scotland*, Edinburgh: Birthlink

Clapton, G. (2007) 'The experiences and needs of birth fathers in adoption: What we know now and some practice implications', *Practice*, Vol. 19, No. 1, pp. 61–71

Clapton, G. (2008) 'The right to information in practice: Adoptions records, confidentiality and secrecy', in Clark, C. and McGhee, J. (eds) (2008) *Private and Confidential? Handling Personal Information in the Social and Health Services*, Bristol: The Policy Press

Clapton, G. (2010) *Relatively Clear: A Search Guide for Adopted Adults in Scotland*, Edinburgh: Birthlink

Coakley, F. and Berrick, J. (2008) 'Research review: In a rush to permanency: Preventing adoption disruption', *Child & Family Social Work*, Vol. 13, pp. 101–12

Collins, J. and Foley, P. (eds) (2008) *Promoting Children's Wellbeing, Policy and Practice*, Bristol: The Policy Press and The Open University

Commission for Social Care Inspection (2006) *About Adoption: A Children's Views Report*, Newcastle upon Tyne: Commission for Social Care Inspection

D'Andrade, A., Frame, L. and Berrick, J. (2006) 'Concurrent planning in public child welfare agencies: Oxymoron or work in progress?' *Children and Youth Services Review*, Vol. 28, No. 1, pp. 78–95

DCSF (2007) *Children Looked After in England (Including Adoption and Care Leavers) Year Ending 31 March 2007*. Available from URL: www.dfes.gov.uk/ rsgateway/DB/SFR/s000741/index.shtml (accessed 18 July 2011)

DCSF (2008) *Adoption: Access to Information and Intermediary Services — Practice Guidance*, Nottingham: Department for Children, Schools and Families

Department for Education and Skills (2006) *Care Matters: Transforming the Lives of Children and Young People in Care*, London: Her Majesty's Stationery Office

Department of Education and Children's Services (2011) 'Listen more and assume less too: The views of children and young people in East Lothian', Vol. 2, Haddington: East Lothian Council

Department of Health, Lord Chancellor's Department and Home Office (1992)

Interdepartmental review of adoption law. *Report to Ministers, A Consultation Document*, para 6.1, quoted in Lewis, J. (2004) 'Adoption: The nature of policy shifts in England and Wales, 1972–2002', *International Journal of Law, Policy and the Family*, Vol. 18, No. 2, p. 244

Department of Health (1999) *Adoption Now: Messages from Research*, Chichester: John Wiley

Deykin, E., Campbell, L. and Patti, P. (1984) 'The post adoption experience of surrendering parents', *American Journal of Orthopsychiatry*, Vol. 54, pp. 271–80

Doolan, M., Nixon, P. and Lawrence, P. (2004) *Growing Up in the Care of Relatives and Friends*, London: Family Rights Group/Kinship Care Coalition

Farmer, E, (2010) 'What factors relate to good placement outcomes in kinship care?', *British Journal of Social Work*, Vol. 40, No. 2, pp. 426–44

Feast, J. (2010) 'Access to information: Progress and perils', *Adoption & Fostering*, Vol. 34, No. 3, 74–9

Feast, J., Kyle, F. and Triseliotis, J. (2011) 'Adoptive fathers' experiences of search and reunion', *Adoption & Fostering*, Vol. 35, No. 1, 57–64

Feast, J. and Smith, J. 'Openness and opportunities — review of an intermediary service for birth relatives', *Adoption & Fostering*, Vol. 19, No. 3, pp. 17–23

The Fostering Network (2005) *Caring for Our Children — Fostercare in Scotland*, Edinburgh: Scottish Executive

Gleeson, J. and Seryak, C. (2010) ' "I made some mistakes … but I love them dearly": The views of parents of children in informal kinship care', *Child & Family Social Work*, Vol. 15, pp. 87–96

Goddard, J., Feast, J. and Kirton, D. (2008) 'A childhood on paper: Managing access to child care files by post-care adults', *Adoption & Fostering*, Vol. 32, No. 2, pp. 50–62

Goldstein, J., Freud, A. and Solnit, A. (1973) *Beyond the Best Interests of the Child*, New York: Macmillan

GRO (2009) *Scotland's Population 2008: The Registrar General's Annual Review of Demographic Trends*, Edinburgh: General Register Office

Grotevant, H. and McRoy, R. (1998) *Openness in Adoption: Exploring Family Connections*, Thousand Oaks, Calif.: Sage

Happer, H., McCreadie, J. and Aldgate, J. (2006) *Celebrating Success: What Helps Looked After Children Succeed*, Edinburgh: SWIA

Hill, M. (1989) 'The role of social networks in the care of young children', *Children & Society*, Vol. 3, pp. 195–211

Hill, M. (1992) Book Review, *British Journal of Social Work*, Vol. 22, No. 5, pp. 597–8

Hill, M. (ed.) (2002a) *Shaping Childcare Practice in Scotland*, London: BAAF

Hill, M. (2002b) 'Adoption and fostering in Scotland — contexts and trends', in Hill, M. (ed.) (2002) *Shaping Childcare Practice in Scotland*, London: BAAF, pp. 3–18

Hill, M. (2002c) 'Perspectives on foster care', in Hill. M. (ed.) (2002) *Shaping Childcare Practice in Scotland*, London: BAAF, pp. 283–9

Hill, M. (2002d) 'Trends in child placement philosphy', in Hill, M. (ed.) (2002) *Shaping Childcare Practice in Scotland*, London: BAAF, pp. 19–25

Hill, M. and Shaw, M. (1998) *Signposts in Adoption: Policy, Practice and Research Issues*, London: BAAF

Hill, M., Stafford, A., Seaman, P., Ross, N. and Daniel, B. (2007) *Parenting and Resilience*. York: Joseph Rowntree Foundation

Hill, M. and Triseliotis, J. (1986) 'Adoption allowances in Scotland', *Adoption & Fostering*, Vol. 10, No. 4, pp. 11–19

Hoggan, P. (1991) 'Attitudes to post-placement support services in permanent family placement', *Adoption & Fostering*, Vol. 15, No. 1, pp. 28–30

Hothersall, S. (2008) *Social Work with Children, Young People and Their Families in Scotland*, 2nd edn, Exeter: Learning Matters

Howe, D. and Feast, J. (2000) *Adoption, Search and Reunion*, London: The Children's Society

Howe, D. and Feast, J. (2001) 'The long-term outcomes of reunions between adult adopted people and their birth mothers', *British Journal of Social Work*, Vol. 31, No. 3, pp. 351–68

Howe, D. and Feast, J. (2004) *Adoption Search and Reunion: The Long-term Experience of Adopted Adults*, London: BAAF

Howe, D., Sawbridge, P. and Hinings, D. (1992) *Half a Million Women: Mothers Who Lose Their Children by Adoption*, London: Penguin

Howe, D., Shemmings, D. and Feast, J. (2001) 'Age at placement and adult adopted people's experience of being adopted', *Child & Family Social Work*, Vol. 6, No. 4, pp. 337–49

Hughes, B. and Logan, J. (1993) *Birth Parents: The Hidden Dimension*, Manchester: University of Manchester

Hunt, J. (2009) Editorial, *Adoption & Fostering*, Vol. 33, No. 3, pp. 2–5

Inverclyde Child Protection Committee (2008) *Summary Annual Report 2007–8 and Business Plan 2008–9*, Gourock: Inverclyde Council. Available at URL: www.inverclyde.gov.uk (accessed 3 March 2011)

Iredale, S. and Staples, M. (1997) *Reunions: True Stories of Adoptees Meeting with Their Natural Parents*, London: The Adoption Society

Jackson, S. (2007) 'Progress at last?', *Adoption & Fostering*, Vol. 31, No. 1 (special edn devoted to educational outcomes), pp. 3–5

Jenkins, S. and Norman, E. (1972) *Filial Deprivation and Foster Care*, New York and London: Columbia University Press

Kay, J. (2000) *The Adoption Papers*, Northumberland: Bloodaxe Books

Kay, J. (2010) *Red Dust Road*, London: Picador

Kelly, R. (2006) 'Reflections on adoption reunion', presentation at Second International Conference on Adoption Research, July 2006, University of East Anglia, Norwich

Kelly, G. and Gilligan, R. (2000) *Issues in Foster Care: Policy, Practice and Research*, London: Jessica Kingsley

Kilbrandon Committee (1964) *Report on Children and Young Persons, Scotland*, Edinburgh: HMSO

Leeson, C. (2007) 'My life in care: Experiences of non-participation in decision-making processes', *Child & Family Social Work*, Vol. 12, No. 3, pp. 268–77

Little, M. (2005) 'Time for a change: A review of Fostering Now and other programmes of research on children in need', *Adoption & Fostering*, Vol. 29,

No. 4, pp. 9–22

Macaskill, C. (1988) 'It's been a bonus — families' experience of adopting children with disabilities', *Adoption & Fostering*, Vol. 12, No. 2, pp. 24–30

Mackay, N. (2003) 'Revealed: The scandal of Scotland's lost children', *The Sunday Herald*, 26 January

Maclean, K. and Hudson, B. (2010) 'Fostering and adoption in Scotland 1980–2010', *Adoption & Fostering*, Vol. 34, No. 3, pp. 21–5

McLeod, A. (2010) 'Thirty years of listening to children?', *Adoption & Fostering*, Vol. 34, No. 3, pp. 67–73

McRoy, R, (1991) 'American experience and research on openness', *Adoption & Fostering*, Vol. 15, No. 4, pp. 99–111

Marsh, P. and Thoburn, J. (2002) 'Policy digest: The adoption and permanence debate in England and Wales', *Child & Family Social Work*, Vol. 7, No. 2, pp. 131–2

Moyers, S., Farmer, E. and Lipscombe, J. (2006) 'Contact with family members and its impact on adolescents and their foster placements', *British Journal of Social Work*, Vol. 36, No. 4, pp. 541–59

Neil, E. (2000) 'The reasons why young children are placed for adoption: Findings from a recently placed sample and a discussion of implications for subsequent identity development', *Child & Family Social Work*, Vol. 5, No. 4, pp. 303–16

Neil, E. (2002) 'Contact after adoption: The role of agencies in making and supporting plans', *Adoption & Fostering*, Vol. 26, No. 1, pp. 25–38

Neil, E. (2009) 'Post-adoption contact and openness in adoptive parents' minds: Consequences for children's development', *British Journal of Social Work*, Vol. 39, No. 1, pp. 5–23

North Lanarkshire Education Psycholoogy Service (2008), 'Our future in your hands', presentation and handout at a North Lanarkshire Children's Partnership Conference in October 2008

Palmer, H. (2009) 'BAAF health group conference 2008 — A child's family health legacy', *Adoption & Fostering*, Vol. 32, No. 4, pp. 85–8

Parker, E. (2006) *Children Social Policy: 'Identity, Rhetoric and Reality'*, Social Work Monograph 220, Norwich: University of East Anglia

Parker, R. (1999) *Adoption Now: Messages from Research*, Chichester: Wiley

Parliament of Australia (2004) *Inquiry into Children in Institutional Care*, Canberra: Parliament of Australia. Available at URL: www.aph.gov.au/senate/committee/clac_ctte/completed_inquiries/2004-07/inst_care/index.htm (accessed 5 August 2011)

Phillips R. (2007) 'The need for information on how the attachment difficulties of adopted and looked after children affect their schooling', *Adoption & Fostering*, Vol. 31, No. 3, pp. 28–38

PIU (2000) *The Prime Minister's Review of Adoption*, London: Performance and Innovation Unit. Available at URL: s3.amazonaws.com/zanran_storage/www.cabinetoffice.gov.uk/ContentPages/27154697.pdf (accessed 5 August 2011)

Prior, V. and Glaser, D. (2006) *Understanding Attachment and Attachment Disorders: Theory, Evidence and Practice*, London: Jessica Kingsley

Quinton, D., Rushton, A., Dance, C. and Mayes, D. (1997) 'Contact between children placed away from home and their birth parents: Research issues and evidence', *Clinical Child Psychology and Psychiatry*, Vol. 2, No. 3, pp. 393–413

Quinton D., Selwyn, J., Rushton, A. and Dance, C. (1999) 'Contact between children placed away from home and their parents: Ryburn's reanalysis analysed', *Clinical Child Psychology and Psychiatry*, Vol. 4, No. 4, pp. 519–31

Randall, J. (2009) 'Towards a better understanding of the needs of children currently adopted from care: An analysis of placements 2003–2005', *Adoption & Fostering*, Vol. 33, No. 1, pp. 44–55

Revans, L. (2007) 'Care leavers who are now adults seek access to information', *Community Care*, 18 July, pp. 18–19

Robinson, C. and Stalker, K. (eds) (1998) *Growing Up with Disability*, London: Jessica Kingsley

Robinson, E. (2010) *Adoption Separation — Then and Now*, South Australia: Clova Books

Rowe, J. and Lambert, L. (1973) *Children Who Wait: A Study of Children Needing Substitute Families*, London: Association of British Adoption Agencies

Rushbrooke, R. (2001) 'The proportion of adoptees who have received their birth records in England and Wales', *Population Trends, 104*, Newport, South Wales: Office of National Statistics, pp. 26–34. Available at URL: www.statistics.gov.uk/articles/population_trends/adopteebirthrec_pt104.pdf (accessed 5 August 2011)

Rushton, A. (2004) 'A scoping and scanning review of research on the adoption of children placed from public care', *Clinical Child Psychology and Psychiatry*, Vol. 9, No. 1, pp. 89–106

Ryburn, M. (1999) 'Contact between children placed away from home and their birth parents: A re-analysis of the evidence in relation to permanent placements', *Clinical Child Psychology and Psychiatry*, Vol. 4, No. 4, pp. 505–18

Schofield, G, (2003) *Part of the Family: Pathways Through Foster Care*, London: BAAF

SCIE (2003) *Innovative, Tried and Tested: A Review of Good Practice in Fostering*, London: Social Care Institute for Excellence

SCIE (2004a) *Promoting resilience in fostered children and young people*, London: Social Care Institute for Excellence

SCIE (2004b) *Guide 7 — Fostering*, London: Social Care Institute for Excellence

Scottish Adoption (2006) *Adopted Children Everywhere in Scotland*, Submission to Education Committee, during passage of Adoption and Children (Scotland) Bill (ED/S2/06/14/1). Available at URL: www.scottish.parliament.uk/business/committees/education/inquiries/adopt/ed06-adoptionbill-evid.htm (accessed 5 August 2011)

Scottish Commission for the Regulation of Care (2007) *The Quality of Fostering and Adoption Services in Scotland*, Dundee: Care Commission

Scottish Commissioner for Children and Young People (2008) *Sweet 16? The Age of Leaving Care in Scotland*, Edinburgh: SCCYP

Scottish Executive (2001) *Getting Our Priorities Right*, Edinburgh: Scottish Executive

Scottish Executive (2002) *Adoption Policy Review Group — Report Phase I*,

Edinburgh: Scottish Executive

Scottish Executive (2005) *Adoption: Better Choices for Our Children, Adoption Policy Review Group: Report of Phase II*, Edinburgh: Scottish Executive

Scottish Executive (2006) *The Adoption and Children (Scotland) Bill Policy Memorandum*, Edinburgh: Scottish Executive

Scottish Executive (2007) *Looked After Children and Young People: We Can and Must Do Better*, Edinburgh: Scottish Executive

Scottish Government (2007) *Getting It Right for Every Child in Kinship and Foster Care*, Edinburgh: Scottish Government. Available at URL: www.scotland.gov.uk/Topics/People/Young-People/childrensservices/girfec (accessed 5 August 2011)

Scottish Government (2008a) *A Guide to Getting It Right for Every Child*, Edinburgh: Scottish Government. Available at URL: www.scotland.gov.uk/Publications/2008/09/22091734/0/Q/ViewArchived/On (accessed 5 August 2011)

Scottish Government (2008b) *These Are Our Bairns: A Guide for Community Planning Partnerships on Being a Good Corporate Parent*, Edinburgh: Scottish Government

Scottish Government (2008c) *Moving Forward in Kinship and Foster Care: Final Report on the GIRFEC in Kinship and Foster Care Strategy*, Edinburgh: Scottish Government

Scottish Government (2008d) *Guidance To Local Authorities on the Assessment and Support for Kinship Carers of Looked After Children*, Scottish Government

Scottish Government (2008e) *The Early Years [0–8] Framework*, Edinburgh: Scottish Government

Scottish Government (2008f) *National Care Standards Adoption Agencies*, Edinburgh: Scottish Government

Scottish Government (2009a) *Improving Adoption Policy. Available at URL:* www.scotland.gov.uk/Topics/People/Young-People/children-families/17972/10958 (accessed 5 August 2011)

Scottish Government (2009b) *Safer Lives: Changed Lives*, Edinburgh: Scottish Government

Scottish Government (2011a) *Guidance on Looked After Children (Scotland) Regulations 2009 and the Adoption and Children (Scotland) Act 2007*, Edinburgh: Scottish Government

Scottish Government (2011b) *Health and Care Series Children Looked After Statistics.* Available at URL: www.scotland.gov.uk/News/Releases/2011/02/23091516 (accessed 5 August 2011)

Scottish Office (1997) *Scotland's Children: The Children (Scotland) Act 1995, Regulations and Guidance*, Vols 1–3, Edinburgh: HMSO

Scottish Voluntary Adoption Agencies (2009) *A List of the Adoption and Support Services provided by Scottish Voluntary Adoption Agencies*, Edinburgh: Scottish Voluntary Adoption Agencies

SCRA (2010) *Changing for Children*, Scottish Children's Reporter Administration Annual Report, 2009/10). Available at URL: www.scra.gov.uk/cms_resources/Annual Report 2009-2010 web.pdf (accessed 5 August 2011

Sellick, C. (2007) 'An examination of adoption support services for birth relatives and for post-adoption contact in England and Wales', *Adoption &*

Fostering, Vol. 31, No. 4, pp. 17–26

Sellick, C. and Thoburn, J. (1996) *What Works in Family Placement*, Barking-side, Barnardos

Selman, P. (1999) 'In search of origins: Estimating lifetime take up of access to birth records in England', poster presentation at International Conference on Adoption Research, Minneapolis, 10–14 August

Selwyn, J. and Quinton, D. (2004) 'Stability, permanence, outcomes and support: Foster care and adoption compared', *Adoption & Fostering*, Vol. 28, No. 4, pp. 6–15

Shaw, T. (2007) *Historical Abuse Systemic Review: Residential Schools and Children's Homes in Scotland 1950 to 1995*, Edinburgh: Scottish Government

Shawyer, J. (1979) *Death by Adoption*, Sydney, Australia: Cicada

Sim, M. and O'Hara, G. (1982) 'Group work with children who are joining new families', *Adoption & Fostering*, Vol. 6, No. 4, pp. 31–7

Singh, S. (1997) 'Assessing Asian families in Scotland — a discussion', *Adoption & Fostering*, Vol. 21, No. 2, pp. 35–9

Singh, S. (2005) *Beyond Caring: An Examination of the Circumstances of 'Looked After' Black and Minority Ethnic Children in Scotland*, Edinburgh: British Association for Adoption & Fostering

The Skinner Report (1992) *Another Kind of Home: A Review of Residential Child Care*, Report of committee chaired by Angus Skinner, Edinburgh: HMSO

Smith, C. and Logan, J. (2004) *After Adoption: Direct Contact and Relationships*, London: Routledge

Stein, M. (2006) 'Research review: Young people leaving care', *Child & Family Social Work*, Vol. 11, No. 3, pp. 273–9

Sullivan, R. and Lathrop, E. (2004) 'Openness in adoption: Retrospective issues and prospective choices', *Children and Youth Services Review*, Vol. 26, No. 4, pp. 393–411

SWIA (2005) *An Inspection into the Care and Protection of Children in Eilean Siar*, Edinburgh: Scottish Executive

SWIA (2006) *Extraordinary Lives — Creating a Positive Future for Looked After Children and Young People in Scotland*, Edinburgh: Social Work Inspection Agency

Tarara, H. and Daniel, B. (2007) *Audit of Scottish Child Care and Protection Research: 1997–2007, Summary*. Available at URL: www.sccpn.stir.ac.uk (accessed 18 July 2011)

Thoburn, J. (2003) 'The risks and rewards of adoption for children in the public care', *Child and Family Law Quarterly*, Vol. 15, No. 4, pp. 391–401

Thomas, C. and Beckford, V. with Murch, M. and Lowe, N. (1999) *Adopted Children Speaking*, London: BAAF

Thorpe, R. (1980) 'The experiences of children and parents living apart: Implications and guidelines for practice', in Triseliotis, J. (ed.) (1980) *New Developments in Foster Care and Adoption*, London: Routledge & Kegan Paul

Trinder, E., Feast, J. and Howe, D. (2004) *The Adoption Reunion Handbook*, Chichester: John Wiley

Triseliotis, J. *(1973) In Search of Origins*, London: Routledge & Kegan Paul

Triseliotis, J. (2010) 'Contact between looked after children and their parents: A level playing field?', *Adoption & Fostering*, Vol. 34, No. 3, pp. 59–66

Triseliotis, J., Borland, M. and Hill, M. (1999) *Fostering Good Relations: A Study of Foster Care and Foster Carers in Scotland*, Edinburgh: Scottish Executive Central Research Unit. Available at URL: http: www.scotland.gov.uk/ Publications/1999/10/856841b9-a428-4dc6-b53a-cd737fe34078 (accessed 5 August 2011)

Triseliotis, J., Feast, J. and Kyle, F. (2005) *The Adoption Triangle Revisited: A Study of Adoption, Search and Reunion Experience*, London: BAAF

Ward, H. and Skuse, T. (2001) 'Performance targets and stability of placements for children long looked after away from home', *Children & Society*, Vol. 15, pp. 333–46

Who Cares? Scotland (2009) *Reaching Higher: Who Cares? Scotland Annual Review 2008/9*, Glasgow: Who Cares? Scotland

Who Cares? Scotland (2010) *Annual Review 2009/10*, Glasgow: Who Cares? Scotland

Wilson, K., Fyson, R. and Newstone, S. (2007) 'Foster fathers: Their experiences and contributions to fostering', *Child & Family Social Work*, Vol. 12, No. 1 pp. 22–31

Winkler, R. and van Keppel, M. (1984) *Relinquishing Mothers in Adoption: Their Long-Term Adjustment*, Melbourne: Institute of Family Studies

Witney, C. (2005) 'Over half a million fathers: An exploration into the experiences of fathers involved in adoption in the mid-twentieth century in England and Wales', *Journal of Social Work*, Vol. 5, No. 1, pp. 83–99

Wolfgram, S. (2008) 'Openness in adoption: What we know so far: A critical review of the literature', *Social Work*, Vol. 53, No. 2, pp.133–42

Further Reading

Brodzinsky, David and Schechter, Marshall D. (1990) *The Psychology of Adoption*, Oxford: Oxford University Press

Commission for Social Care Inspection (2006) *About Adoption: A Children's Views Report*, London: Commission for Social Care Inspection

Daniel, Brigid, Wassell, Sally and Campbell, Iain (2002) *The Early Years: Assessing and Promoting Resilience in Vulnerable Children*, London: Jessica Kingsley

Fahlberg, Vera (2004) *A Child's Journey Through Placement*, London: BAAF

Gilligan, Robbie (2009) *Promoting Resilience*, London: BAAF

Plumtree, Alexandra (2011) *Permanence and Adoption for Children: A Guide to the Adoption and Children (Scotland) Act*, London: BAAF

Rutter, Michael (2005) *Child and Adolescent Psychiatry*, 4th edn, Chichester: Wiley

Scottish Commissioner for Children and Young People (2008) *Sweet 16? The Age of Leaving Care in Scotland*, Edinburgh: SCCYP

Smith, Fergus and Stewart, Roy with Stobie, Alistair (2011) *Adoption and Children (Scotland) Act: The Act and Regulations*, London: BAAF

The Care Leavers Association (2010) *Listen Up! Adult Care Leavers Speak Out*, Manchester: The Care Leavers Association

Verrier, Nancy (2004) *The Primal Wound: Understanding the Adopted Child*, Lafayette, Calif.: Verrier Publishing

INDEX

Note: page numbers in *italics* denote figures or tables